White Sail

WHITE SAIL

Crossing the Waves
of Ocean Mind to the
Serene Continent of
the Triple Gems

Thinley Norbu

SHAMBHALA
Boston & London
1992

Shambhala Publications, Inc.
Horticultural Hall
300 Massachusetts Avenue
Boston, Massachusetts 02115

9 8 7 6 5 4 3 2

Printed in the United States of Ameria on acid-free paper ∞
Distributed in the United States by Random House, Inc.,
and in Canada by Random House of Canada Ltd.

Library of Congress Cataloging-in-Publication Data
Thinley Norbu.
White sail: crossing the waves of ocean mind to the serene
continent of the triple gems / Thinley Norbu—1st ed.
p.   cm.
ISBN 0-87773-693-6 (paperback original: acid-free paper)
1. Buddhism—Doctrines.   2. Religious life—Buddhism.   1. Title.
BQ4150.T48   1992   92-50129
294.3'42—dc20   CIP

While briefly lent this precious human body's white sail
Pushed by clean intention's gentle wind
Without turning back toward miserable samsaric deserts
And making the error of missing this chance
Try to receive virtue's jewels by crossing the waves of
    ocean mind
To the serene continent of the Triple Gems
Since doing this is more meaningful than anything else

Contents

Offering Praise

All beings are aroused from the darkness of ignorant sleep
By the youthful, sun-colored dawn of your entrancing,
    noble body.
The ego net of their dualism is slashed into stainless
    awareness
By just raising your awesome, keen, flaming wisdom
    sword.
Most all-knowing Mañjuśrī,
I, the one named Jewel of Activity,
With amaranthine faith,
Offer ornaments to adorn you.
Please illuminate the radiant wisdom spirit
Of my precious Buddha nature.

All beings' sorrowful twilight miseries are dispelled
By the moonbeams of your serenely exquisite wisdom
    body.
Even the lyrical song of young beloveds' heartwhispering
Cannot be compared to the soothing, resonant melody of
    your delicately fingered, celestial tamboura
That awakens the dusky habit of dullness into harmonious
    awareness.
Most comforting of comforters, Saraswatī,
I, the one named Jewel of Activity,
With amaranthine faith,
Offer ornaments to adorn you.
Please illuminate the radiant wisdom spirit
Of my precious Buddha nature.

All beings' endless karmic defilements are purified
By just seeing the perfection of your pearl rosary smile.
The murky swamp of saṃsāra is cleansed
By the flowing crystal waves
Of your pristine treasure river of knowledge.
Most kind of kind Buddhas,
Our guide in this degenerate age, Buddha Śakyamuni,
I, the one named Jewel of Activity,
With amaranthine faith,
Offer ornaments to adorn you.
Please illuminate the radiant wisdom spirit
Of my precious Buddha nature.

All fortunate beings are guided on the miraculous path to
    the lotus field of Buddha Amitabha
By the blessing of your divine, magical activity.
The longing and sadness of all samsaric reminiscence cease
By just remembering your glorious, blossoming lotus face.
Embodiment of ineffable wisdom ecstasy of all Buddhas
    and diadem of all saints,
Wisdom dakinis surround you, flowering with flawless
    exaltation.
Most wondrous lotus-born vajramaster, Padmasambhava,
I, the one named Jewel of Activity,
With amaranthine faith,
Offer ornaments to adorn you.
Please illuminate the radiant wisdom spirit
Of my precious Buddha nature.

All beings, desperate orphans lost in saṃsāra's wilderness
    from lack of faith,
Are nurtured and enlivened by the vast panacea of the milk
    of your unconditioned love.

You prayed and prayed to emanate in countless feminine
  manifestations to create Triple Gems' appearances for
  all beings,
Leading them to purelands beautified with unfading trees
  of turquoise leaves.
Wisdom mother of all Buddhas and Bodhisattvas, great
  liberator Ārya Tārā,
You appear again as the inexpressible great bliss wisdom
  consort of Padmasambhava and supreme treasure
  holder of his speech.
Most compassionate Yeshe Tshogyal,
I, the one named Jewel of Activity,
With amaranthine faith,
Offer ornaments to adorn you.
Please illuminate the radiant wisdom spirit
Of my precious Buddha nature.

Preface

Those who truly intend to benefit others
    through holy teachings
Do not use elaborate terms and poetry.
The pure path is shown with the simple
    words of the laity.
That is the sublime method of the Bodhi-
    sattvas.
— GLORIOUS EMANATION JEWEL, FEARLESS
    POWER OF DHARMA, PATRUL RINPOCHE,
    JIGMED CHHÖKYI WANGPO

At many different times and in many different places, many people have asked me questions. This book is composed of a few of the answers, such as the answer to Roger Weil's request to establish the basis for learning how to enliven and increase positive phenomena by transforming the limited, tangible, finite deception of the nihilist delusion into the vast, intangible, infinite appearances of enlightenment. There are also other subjects which are answers to other people's questions about sectarianism and nonsectarianism, philosophy, karma, faith, the basic idea of deities, the kāyas, and so on.

The nihilist point of view is often mentioned in this book in order to show what it actually is. This is not done for the purpose of insulting nihilists. According to the Mahāyāna teachings, all sentient beings have Buddha nature and are potentially and ultimately the same as Buddha, whether they are nihilists, eternalists, or Buddhists. In order to show people how to recognize Buddha so they can keep from building and remaining in nihilist habits for many lives, it is explained with good intention what it means not to believe in the immeasurable qualities of wisdom spirituality. But some people who are loyal to their strong, karmic, nihilist habits and have misconceptions about spirituality may think this book is too critical.

Buddhists have always analyzed the differences between the doctrines of nihilism and eternalism in order to establish the point of view of Buddhist philosophical teachings and to guide us to the path of enlightenment. This is not done to deprecate others or to build one's own Buddhist ego, but only to liberate all sentient beings through impartial compassion from the views of these two extremes to enlightenment.

For those of us who are trying to practice Buddhism, it is important to introspect and identify the nihilist habit of our own minds. Then we can watch this habit and see that it does not make sense. There is no reason not to believe in anything. Instead of defending a nihilist point of view that has no ultimate benefit, we had better try to believe in Buddha nature and let wisdom blossom for the benefit of the enlightenment of all beings.

Sublime beings of ancient times have left many noble signs of their activity as examples for us to follow, so that we can open our wisdom energy and qualities. But because of nihilist habit, most people have closed minds and do not want to hear even one word of their precious teachings.

Some of us like to hear and read their teachings, but if our intention is not pure, we only think of them as temporarily interesting and use them for ordinary purposes, such as intellectual entertainment. Because of this, there is probably no benefit in writing. Patrul Rinpoche said:

> Hundreds of ordinary and sublime beings from ancient times
> Have all left their theories in the world.
> But in the minds of children, contradiction always increases
>   instead of benefit.
> So, for anyone who leaves new theories, it will be the same.

Even though we would like to increase wisdom qualities, a connection can very rarely be made between the object which is the nectar of the holy teachings of Buddha, and the subject which is the container of sentient beings' minds. This is because two mistakes are usually made. One mistake is aversion to tradition, caused by the habit of freedom, which is like wanting to cross to the other shore of a river but not wanting to depend on a boat. Without any point of view or realization, the rejection of tradition can prevent the development of spiritual qualities, since there will not be any focus or method of recognition. The other mistake is tightly grasping at tradition, caused by the habit of restraint, which is like aiming for the top of a high tower but being stuck on a ladder. The significance of tradition is misinterpreted by trying to turn it into the ultimate target. Also, if we try to make our own tradition important because we want to be more special than others, we will just be building ordinary power with a self-righteous ego.

Some of us are not interested in following in the footsteps of sublime beings. Even when we hear their histories, we may think they are not relevant to our lives because we do not see that there is always a natural connection between our minds and sublime beings. But if we distance ourselves from them and their wonderful histories, we only create discouragement.

Some of us want to increase pure spiritual energy with good intention, but misunderstand the deep meaning of sublime beings. Either we cannot connect with them because of our disbelief and lack of reverence and faith, or our reverence is twisted into an exaggerated respect for tradition, which turns tradition itself into a tangible, worldly object. Then, because this perpetuates the division between subject and object, actual, nondualistic, spiritual qualities never develop. The objects of our perception remain ordinary objects, the subjectivity of our ego remains an ordinary subject, and both remain inert without the lively, reliable, intangible energy of pure appearance. In this way, we create ordinary, unreliable, fragmented energy instead of sublime, uplifting, continuous wisdom energy.

Many of us feel threatened by religious teachings, including the precious teachings of the Buddhas, because we cannot fit their vast qualities into our narrow minds. But there is nothing to fear. The Buddhas and their precious teachings are the self-secret, constant companion which is the cause of open, unobstructed light energy. However, we are always afraid of light. Even though we may not realize it, we are afraid that we will lose ourselves if we change our rigid, heavy habit of grasping at substance. We do not realize that we are continuously losing because of the impermanent nature of substance, and our constant concern with losing is the cause of constant suffering.

In this book, I have tried to explain the characteristics of tangible, nihilist ideas and intangible, spiritual wisdom qualities which are the essence of both the tangible and intangible. Through the experience of each individual's self-logic, and through the rare and precious teachings of the Buddha, the connection can be made from the material to the immaterial, spiritual qualities inherent in the minds of all beings.

I dedicate this book to all sentient beings, including my friends who have helped me in many ways, always sustaining themselves without contradiction between tangible and intangible inexpressible appearance.

White Sail

Introduction

I show you the path of liberation.
Whether you attain liberation is up to you.

— LORD BUDDHA

From the beginningless beginning, the essence of nondualistic wisdom mind is pure and stainless like a mirror. All measureless phenomena can arise through this unobstructed, mirrorlike quality without causing division between subject and object. Without division between subject and object, there is no grasping or clinging and there are no temporary circumstances, so all manifestation is wisdom display.

From the beginningless beginning, the essence of all sentient beings' minds is the same as the Buddha's nondualistic wisdom mind, pure and stainless like a mirror. But we ordinary sentient beings do not recognize this pure and stainless wisdom mind because we divide its reflections into subject and object. By grasping and clinging to subject and object, we prevent ourselves from recognizing the continuous display of wisdom. Actually, since mind's essence is pure, obscurations do not exist. But through our misinterpretation of all phenomena as real and tangible, they become temporary obscurations which trap us.

As Omniscient Great Profound Supreme Expanse, Kunkhyen Longchen Rabjam, said:

Self-arising awareness, the absolute sun,
Is obscured by both white and black clouds of virtue and
nonvirtue.

3

The effort of attachment to acceptance and rejection is a tur-
    bulent lightning storm.
The rainfall of delusion's happiness and suffering continuously
    descends;
Saṃsāra's seed produces the abundantly growing crops of the
    six realms.
Alas! All tormented sentient beings are pitiful.

According to the Buddhist point of view, intangible mind exists
from the beginningless beginning. This does not mean from the beginning of ego in just one life, but means that it exists continuously,
as the basis of all phenomena, until wisdom mind is realized and
full enlightenment is reached. But through our misinterpretation,
we cause habits which produce different realms of phenomena. The
hell realm is created predominantly through the habit of hatred;
the hungry ghost realm is created predominantly through the habit
of greed; the animal realm is created predominantly through the
habit of ignorance; the jealous god realm is created predominantly
through the habit of jealousy; the god realm is created predominantly through the habit of pride; and the human realm is created
predominantly through the habit of desire.

Among human beings, the nihilist view is created predominantly
from the pessimistic habit of believing in nothing beyond the tangible
qualities of what is experienced through this life's ego. The eternalist
view is created predominantly from the optimistic habit of believing
in a supreme, eternal god. The Buddhist view goes beyond both nihilism and eternalism.

Buddhists believe that all phenomena originate from, and are inseparable from, great emptiness. Great emptiness means the limitless,
stainless, unobscured, spacious origin of all wisdom qualities. Great
stainless emptiness wisdom mind contains and creates all wisdom appearances and qualities through great space. The three aspects of Buddha's qualities of wisdom body, speech, and mind are the pure appearance of wisdom mind's display.

4

Buddha's wisdom body is inconceivably secret. It can never be defined because it has no limitation. It reflects any form unobstructedly in infinite aspects, so ordinary beings cannot find an end to its appearances. Since the source is inconceivable, the aspects are inexhaustible.

Buddha's wisdom speech is inconceivably secret. It can never be judged because its quality is so profound. It reflects any sound unobstructedly in infinite aspects, so ordinary beings cannot find an end to its expressions. Since the source is inconceivable, the aspects are inexhaustible.

Buddha's wisdom mind is inconceivably secret. It can never be known because it is beyond dualistic mind. It reflects immeasurable knowledge unobstructedly in infinite aspects, so ordinary beings cannot find an end to its omniscience. Since the source is inconceivable, the aspects are inexhaustible.

Different Thoughts

If we do not believe in what we cannot see, it does not mean that it does not exist. If someone is blind, he cannot see anything, but this does not mean that what he cannot see does not exist, since it can be seen by others.

If we do not believe in what we cannot hear, it does not mean that it does not exist. If someone is deaf, he cannot hear anything, but this does not mean that what he cannot hear does not exist, since it can be heard by others.

If we do not believe in what we cannot say, it does not mean that it does not exist. If someone is mute, he cannot say anything, but this does not mean that what he cannot say does not exist, since it can be said by others.

The nihilist point of view is one of the biggest problems for all beings. It only relies on trusting temporary circumstances that cannot be depended on any more than a prostitute can depend on the uncertain appearance of her customers. Since the nihilist point of view distorts perception through its singular focus on substance, intangible spiritual phenomena cannot be seen clearly and intangible continuous mind cannot be recognized.

Even if we do not accept that mind is continuous, we still believe that consciousness can exist as long as the circumstances appear which produce it. But if consciousness is only used to respond to circumstances, we feel unhappy when negative circumstances arise, we feel happy when positive circumstances arise, and our existence becomes just a reaction to what happens from moment to moment. By thinking that it is only this circumstance-dependent consciousness that creates our countless conceptions, we do not recognize their intangible source in continuous mind.

We may say we can only believe in what can be experienced or proven, but actually we believe selectively in what we have not experienced or proven as long as it is compatible with our other conceptions. We accept and use intangible abstractions of intangible times, places, and circumstances to support what we think is tangibly true, turning the intangible to the tangible through our conception. Because we are only interested in our own version of reality, we miss the potential opportunity to connect tangible qualities to intangible qualities through wisdom's influence.

Without acknowledging mind's continuity, we may think that the consciousness of one fragmented instant only connects to the consciousness of another fragmented instant through the fragmented conceptions of momentary past memory and momentary future plans. But even if we believe that the past is finished or that the future is unreal, we see that there is a mind or perceiver that remembers past experiences and a mind that imagines future experiences, that continues into today and tomorrow until death. If we have had a bad experience in the past, we remember it and try not to repeat the mistake in the future. This is actually accepting that mind connects with the past and future continuously. Both intangible past memories and intangible future plans appear to us again and again, relying on the continuity of our conceptions, which occur unceasingly. We may believe that memory is the source of the continuity of our minds and our capacity to remember and anticipate, but it is actually the continuity of mind that is the true source of memory. Since our ordinary memory is discontinuous and temporary, there is always forgetfulness between memories. These ordinary memories are ultimately meaningless. If instead we use our memory to remember pure Buddha phenomena, we can develop continuous mindfulness which can unveil the basic continuity of mind.

We may say we cannot believe in continuous mind because we cannot perceive it, yet we believe with conviction in the continuity of our conceptions. We are certain that the past becomes the present and the present becomes the future. Actually, we are never disconnected from continuous mind, and we are always using ideas that reflect the mind's continuity. But by trying to locate ourselves somewhere tangibly within time, we prevent ourselves from recognizing this continuity and opening to natural awareness. There is an old Himalayan saying that while being born, there is no memory of making love, and while making love, there is no memory of being born. If we recognize pure, transparent, continuous mind, we can clearly see past and future lifetimes which show this continuity in the same way that we clearly see what is happening to us now. But because we do not perceive it, we do not believe it. Even though enlightenment can be attained through practice, if we do not believe in practice because we do not accept continuous mind, we are automatically prevented from using our actually uninterrupted connection to continuous mind and our potential to increase inexhaustible, pure, spiritual power by transforming this continuity into its pure essence. When we shield ourselves in this way from perceiving anything that contradicts what we already accept as true, we only maintain our nihilist point of view.

There are many different points of view within nihilism, but they all have in common a basic disbelief in the continuity of mind. The consciousness of sentient beings is considered to be a momentary, biological development that occurs as a random event and depends on ephemeral circumstances which arise by chance. Since mind is thought of as only a collection of temporary inner and outer phenomena which ceases at death, the only continuity of mind accepted in nihilism is within the duration of the lifetime of a sentient being.

There are many different points of view within eternalism, but they all unknowingly have in common a basic belief in the continuity of mind, even though they do not call it by this name. They acknowledge the permanence of eternal, continuous gods and the continuity of existence beyond death for those who have faith in those gods.

They believe that the negative and positive consequences of their actions, which they experience in this lifetime and after death, come from gods or supernatural beings. This demonstrates a belief in the continuity of mind until an ultimate destiny is reached. Since this is not a belief in the negation of nothingness, it is much more positive than any nihilist point of view.

There are many different points of view within the different doctrines of Buddhism, but they all have in common a basic belief in the continuity of mind until enlightenment is attained. Whatever exists, within form or formlessly, arises from continuous mind. Ordinary continuous mind (sems kyi gyud) is mind that is obscured by delusion. Its continuity means that it does not end unless these dualistic obscurations are purified. By the purification of obscurations, ordinary continuous mind is transformed into its unobscured essence, and one can realize and abide in the unending continuity of nondualistic wisdom mind (nyugmai yeshe).

According to the Hīnayāna Buddhist view, mind continuously creates passions, karma, and suffering through countless lives until the arhat state is attained through meditation and the self ceases in the state of nonself, or enlightened mind, in which there is no more attachment of the ego. Mind is continuous, since it is fundamentally inexhaustible until enlightenment. Followers of the Sūtra teachings of the Hīnayāna call this the continuity of mind.

According to the Yogācāra view of Mahāyāna Buddhism, all immeasurable phenomena are the habits of the basis of mind. Until the continuous basis of mind becomes stainless, self-awakening wisdom, either mind can continuously create the phenomena of saṃsāra, or the obscurations of mind can be purified and merit and wisdom can be accumulated. Therefore, mind is continuous. Followers of the Yogācāra view call this the basis of all phenomena.

According to the Mādhyamika view of Mahāyāna Buddhism, the basis of mind is free from all fabrication and beyond existence and nonexistence, since it is inexpressible Dharmadhātu. Until confidence in realization is attained, mind must be purified of all habitual phe-

9

nomena, and wisdom and merit must be accumulated. Mind is continuous because, when it becomes Dharmakāya, it is unending and timeless. That is why it is called unending wisdom mind. Followers of the Mādhyamika view call this stainless Dharmakāya.

According to the general Vajrayāna Buddhist view, mind is beginninglessly self-born wisdom deity. Wherever there is mind, there is wisdom. Wisdom exists only within mind, and not anywhere else. Mind is only called mind because of delusion. Wisdom is uninfluenced by dualistic delusion and awakened with the quality of indestructible awareness phenomena. Wisdom is inherent in mind until the power of wisdom mind is completely opened. Through believing in self-born wisdom deity, one must try to transform all immeasurable, ordinary, habitual, samsaric phenomena and perceive wisdom deity field. Perceiving is deity, and the perceiver is śūnyatā. This is wisdom deity, which is totally different from supernatural beings or eternalist gods, since it is uninfluenced by individual ego or the objects of ego, because the perceiver is stainless emptiness. Therefore, there is nothing to cause passions or karma, so there is nothing to cause demons, and so all phenomena are seen as wisdom Buddhas. Mind is continuous until that state of the immeasurable, unending, nondualistic wisdom maṇḍala of Buddha appearance is attained, so that is why it is called continuous mind.

In the path of enlightenment, continuous mind becomes an aspect and quality of the power of wisdom. When continuous mind becomes indistinguishable from the emanation of complete, clear wisdom, it becomes its originally stainless purity. Then, continuous mind is transcended, and there is only the manifestation of wisdom display.

In the result of enlightenment, there is only continuous, unending wisdom mind, which means the continuity of wisdom.

Through not recognizing or believing in unending wisdom mind, many different samsaric habits are unnoticeably created from mind's continuity and many different appearances of habit arise. Just as we have dreamtime phenomena at night as a result of our daytime phenomena habit, we have daytime phenomena in this present life's dream as a result of our previous lives' habit. Even if we accept that mind is continuous, if we do not realize unending wisdom mind, it only becomes the basis of habit which causes the circling suffering of saṃsāra. Ordinary continuous mind does not cause anything ultimately positive, but since it is continuous, it cannot be abandoned. Since it cannot be abandoned, if we wish for the cessation of all worldly conception, our only choice is to transform it through meditation into unending, stainless wisdom mind, which means completely untarnished enlightenment. As the Incomparable Wisdom Scholar, Chhogkyi Langpo, said:

> Except for conception, there is not even the name of saṃsāra.
> Whenever you are free from that conception, you are always in
> enlightenment.

If we believe in mind's basic continuity, we can optimistically commit ourselves to creating good habits to increase boundless, pure, spiritual qualities so that we can transform the basic continuity of ordinary mind into the unending continuity of beginningless, pure wisdom. This is the transformation of ordinary conception into pure appearances.

Awareness mind is pure and unobscured by any contradiction, so it is the essence of unending wisdom mind that is everywhere inconceivably. According to the Mādhyamika teachings, this is called the point of view that is free from fabrication, and according to the Tibetan lineage holders of the Nyingma tradition, it is called the primordial purity of inconceivable great emptiness.

But from lack of faith in Buddha nature, beings suffer by not recognizing this. As it says in *The Uttara Tantra* (*Gyud Lama*):

> Beneath the pauper's house,
> There are inexhaustible treasures.
> But the pauper never realizes this,
> And the treasure never says, "I am here."
> Likewise, the treasure of dharmatā,

Which is naturally pure,
Is trapped in ordinary mind,
And beings always suffer in poverty.

New practitioners who misunderstand about practice may wonder why it is necessary to think further about the suffering of samsaric realms, since they already know they exist. They may think that this only adds conceptions and will not make any difference. But everything is conception in saṃsāra.

Without thinking, introspecting, and caring about the six realms, visualizing and experiencing them, we cannot be released from suffering because we do not recognize the nature of beings. So thinking about the negative characteristics of saṃsāra over and over again is done in order to turn the mind away from saṃsāra and toward positive Dharma.

We may ask why it is necessary to add conceptions by thinking about saṃsāra over and over. But this is a mistake, because all conceptions are not the same. Some thoughts are coming from ignorance and cause negative energy, and some thoughts come from alert, awakened awareness mind and cause positive energy. It may sound as though conceptions are all the same, but their essence and result are different. One kind causes harm and one is beneficial. As it is said in the tantras:

Conception is purified from conception.
Existence is purified from existence.

For example, if we get water in our ears, we can get the water out by putting more water in them that joins with the water that is already there so that we can wash it all out. Likewise, any substantial conceptions are purified by conceptions.

Because unending, continuous mind is unobstructed, it reflects infinite aspects of phenomena. All of these phenomena can be contained within the two categories of the phenomena of saṃsāra and the phenomena of nirvāṇa. The sublime tantric vajra masters of the Nyingma tradition revealed many precious explanations for how these phenomena are created, which are contained in the eight spontaneous ways of arising. These can be synthesized into the two entrances.

When, from primordial, beginningless time, sentient beings do not recognize the reflection of the nondualistic, unobstructed power of wisdom mind's display, the entrance to saṃsāra is opened. Then, through dualistic mind, habit is created, and from habit to habit, saṃsāra is created.

Samantabhadra is the origin of all Buddhas from primordial, beginningless time. If we recognize that all phenomena which arise are the manifestation of his stainless, primordial wisdom mind, they are spontaneously liberated. Since this recognition does not create an object in reality, everything is display, opening the entrance to enlightenment.

If we do not recognize wisdom display, which is the causeless manifestation of the clear appearance of great emptiness, we create reality subject and object. Through the reality of subject and object, we create general and personal phenomena. When manifestations of phenomena are perceived in the same way at the same time and place by a group of sentient beings, their shared perception creates the habit of agreement, and this habit becomes the habit of general phenomena. When manifestations of phenomena are perceived differently by individual beings even though they are perceived at the same time and place, their individual perception becomes the habit of personal phenomena. When the creation of many different habits increases the variety of phenomena until personal phenomena are shared by different individuals, it again creates general phenomena.

If we are nihilists, we prefer to remain in our habit of general, nihilist agreement because it is familiar. Then, after the individual, tangible, karmic energy of our body is exhausted, we still retain the personal phenomena of the habit of general phenomena. Therefore, we are reborn again and again with the same habit of general phenomena due to the force of the karmic habit of our own personal reflections.

We may think it is impossible to release ourselves from the heavy habit of general phenomena and to create the lighter habit of the pure, personal phenomena of practice. It may seem that no matter how much we try, we still have dualistic mind's subject and object that cause habit. Without keeping this previous habit which discourages us from practice, we must truly have faith that Buddha nature is within our own mind. We must remember that the Buddhas come at all times to guide us toward enlightenment, and that they are the reflected appearance of our own Buddha nature. We must know that the Buddhas are continuously teaching us according to our own individual faculties.

When we are developing our phenomena of Buddhas according to the path of practice, there still may seem to be subject and object appearing as the Buddhas and we who follow them. However, we are only using subject and object within practice in order to transcend them. This is entirely different from being caught between saṃsāra's subject and object, which always increases suffering. We are joining our mind's pure reflections to the self-originating maṇḍala of enlightened beings, which always increases wisdom qualities.

Desire for what seems to be a positive object, like a comforting friend, may temporarily bring pleasure, but it always ultimately brings suffering and causes karma again. This desire only creates ordinary, heavy habit since there is nothing lasting and beneficial about joining with ordinary friends in an ordinary way. Instead of grasping toward others, we can think of and pray with faith toward Buddhas as our objects of comfort. This creates light, noble habit which purifies our obscurations, even though momentarily we may not be able to see Buddhas due to our previous nihilist habit. Since Buddhas are the manifestation of primordial, unobstructed wisdom mind, their nature is unobstructed compassion, which always connects with us and never causes suffering or karma. With practice, we can subdue the conceptions of ordinary negative subject and object with the interdisplay of positive subject and object, which transforms into inconceivable, undeluded self-manifestations of Buddhas.

If we want to be released from the trap of our heavy personal and general phenomena and from the circle of our nihilist delusion, we must follow Buddhas' teachings and try to transform our habit of delusion into undistorted awareness. Until we have confidence in our own undistorted wisdom mind, we must continuously have faith in the Triple Gems and practice. In order to release our mind from the habit of heavy, general phenomena, we must try to develop and increase the habit of the light, personal phenomena of wisdom deity until the habit of all general and personal phenomena has been completely exhausted into the habitless, naked ease of naturally manifesting deity and clear wisdom sky space.

The Source of Phenomena

Material reality is compounded.
Immaterial unreality is compounded.
Actual nirvāṇa is uncompounded.

— *from* NĀGĀRJUNA'S *speech*

According to Buddhist teachings, all phenomena come from mind. Dualistic mind is the fundamental source of all the impure phenomena of saṃsāra which exist within the three conditions of being born, ceasing, and remaining. Buddha nature, which exists within the mind of each sentient being, is the fundamental source of all pure phenomena when it is free from the three conditions of being born, ceasing, and remaining. These conditions only exist when Buddha nature is not awakened. When Buddha nature becomes free of dualistic mind and totally blossoms in full enlightenment, the three conditions transform into the manifestation of wisdom.

Actual Buddhas are never born because they are always abiding in unborn Dharmakāya; they never cease, because they are always in unceasing Sambhogakāya; and they never remain in limitation, because they are always in never-remaining Nirmāṇakāya. They only seem to be born, remain, and cease as miraculous reflections according to the phenomena of sentient beings. Actually, whatever arises is the naturally pure quality of the manifestation of unobstructed wisdom.

The unobstructed quality of phenomena is the readiness to reflect anything and everything at any time. These reflections can be deluded, clear, few, or many, corresponding to the capacity of the containers of sentient beings' minds, just as the reflections in a mirror depend on whether it is stained, unstained, small, or large. By acknowledging and realizing Buddha nature as the greatest wisdom creator and source of pure phenomena, revealed by Buddha through his teachings, we can create the pure phenomena that lead us to enlightenment's appearance. But if we do not recognize Buddha nature as the innermost essence of all phenomena, then through the nihilist habit of many lives, we misinterpret the unobstructed manifestations that demonstrate its qualities.

If we have the habit of nihilism, we think that whatever appears as the outer elements and the inner containers of all beings, including one's own body, is real and true. When phenomena cease to appear, we think there is nothing, and when phenomena remain, we think they will always be there. Even though we are now in the human realm, if we keep our habitual position of nihilism and do not release ourselves from the perception that these three conditions are real, we will continuously suffer by circling within the many different realms of existence, whether with momentary negative or positive energy.

If we only hold nonspiritual ideas on the nature of phenomena, believing in the reality of the three conditions, the result must always be a misunderstanding about the relationship between subject and object. For example, the general view of material science is to look for meaning within and between objects and only to believe what is found within substance. This produces a continuous misinterpretation of the interactions between subject and object through grasping at a reality based on a division between objects and mind. Existence is seen as separate from mind, like a projection with no projector. This is why nonspiritual science searches for an external, objective source of phenomena using theories about subtle substance, with the idea that someday a fundamental, irreducible source of all the substantial phenomena of reality can be found.

In general, science is the systematic study of substance in the material world. This does not mean only the scientific conceptions of this modern world, because science exists whenever there are conceptions of substantial elements and their phenomena, and whenever there is engagement with the material world and its infinite categories of substance within the elements. From the science of ancient times to the science of today, only the particular aspect of how substance is used changes within time and place, including whether it is harmful or beneficial, depending on the karmic phenomena of sentient beings.

In nonspiritual science, spiritual ideas are not trusted because they are considered to be imaginary and unreal, and therefore without any actual benefit. This idea comes from a strong habit of associating reality with substance, expecting instant, material answers. It is the result of only believing in obvious, momentary appearances and not believing in incognizable, spiritual qualities. In Buddhism, nonspiritual, material ideas are not trusted because they are considered to be based only on compounded substance. Since the nature of substance is to diminish and decay, it can have no actual benefit. It is thought that through being enticed by too much concern with momentary, substantial phenomena, Buddha nature can become dormant for many lives, which prevents reaching enlightenment. Therefore, in general, the points of view of nonspiritual science and Buddhism are basically different.

We cannot always make judgments about either particular scientists or particular Buddhists, since demons can manifest as spiritual beings in order to disturb the teachings of enlightenment, and Buddhas and Bodhisattvas can manifest as nonspiritual scientists to guide beings who are frightened by or disengaged from spiritual ideas, in this way temporarily reflecting sentient beings' wishes by using material energy to ultimately guide them to immaterial enlightenment. It is difficult for anyone other than sublime beings to judge who harms and who benefits other beings through material or immaterial ideas.

According to Buddhism, mind and its objects are continuously related to each other because ordinary mind exists continuously as the source of samsaric existence unless dualistic habit is exhausted through the recognition of Buddha nature, which is nondualistic wisdom. Existence means the occurrence of any and every possibility. But this does not mean that anything that exists is real. If it exists within dualistic habit, it is always delusion.

From the Mahāyāna Buddhist point of view, the phenomena of ordinary reality are the delusions of dualistic mind. But from the materialistic point of view, the phenomena of ordinary reality are trusted as true because dualistic concepts are believed. This is like building a dam for the water of a mirage.

From the Buddhist point of view, nothing exists independently. Everything that arises within sentient beings' phenomena comes from the interdependent connections of circumstances, according to relative truth. Because everything depends on everything else, there is nothing original, and there is no original source of phenomena to be found within a single substance. Whatever is found objectively does not have an independent existence because it is only found between the interdependence of a subject that finds and an object that is found.

Even if we think we have found the origin of phenomena, we are only being deluded by the karmic seeds of new discoveries which are constantly ripening, becoming exhausted, and being replaced through the ripening of other karmic seeds. Yet we continue to be fascinated with trying to define substance, constantly trying to catch it, thinking that we have caught it but then losing it. We are endlessly lured by the material creations of our conceptions. Sublime beings, knowing the characteristics of each phenomenon and the nature of all phenomena, are never lured by anything. They abide in the infinite display of enlightenment's empty appearance without trying to catch anything or being able to be caught.

Even though sublime beings have the power to create any energy of substance within the elements, they have often taught out of compassion how to develop intangible wisdom energy in order to prevent people from betraying themselves with unreliable, substantial phenomena. In Mahāyāna Buddhism, it is taught that both the tangible and intangible elements can be used with skillful methods for the accumulation of virtue. This is done with the intention of alleviating the suffering that is caused by the tangible phenomena of substance in order to create the immaculate wisdom power of inconceivable, intangible enlightenment. This way of using both substantial and insubstantial phenomena for practice is like using wood to create the light of a fire instead of using it to cause more dismal thickets of saṃsāra.

In tantric Buddhism, it is also taught that the substantial and insubstantial elements can be used within spiritual methods of practice. Since whatever sentient beings wish for they can have, the result of common siddhi can be attained with these methods, but the ultimate aim of tantric Buddhism is always supreme siddhi. This is the perfectly accomplished wisdom energy of enlightenment, beyond substance and containing all nonsubstantial accumulations.

When we examine objects, we must rely on a subject, which is our mind, since mind is the source of objects. Through intention, subject and object produce the force of habit, creating the energy of all dualistic phenomena. Not recognizing this results in the confusion of deluded phenomena and the endless compounded habit field of countless previous lives in which beings have projected the infinite sediment of congested energy which is the phenomena of this universe. If we cannot see the relationship between the interdependent projections of our mind and our previous habit of outer phenomena, we cause even more division between phenomena, so that phenomena seem more separate from each other and farther and farther apart from mind. Whatever is separated from mind cannot be used to locate the source of phenomena. If we do not cause this division, then the possibility is always there to recognize that any substantial and nonsubstantial phenomena can be created through interdependent circumstances as a consequence of our intention. If all objects are understood to be projections of the mind, we can recognize that they are the display of the qualities of the mind, so that we are not fooled into thinking they are independent and external.

Any discoveries that are made within science, art, philosophy, and even spiritual conceptions are only the aspects of different habits at different times and in different places, if they are not connected with wisdom qualities. We cannot rely on these discoveries if we are truly interested in attaining enlightenment, because they are only the fluctuating creations of previous karma from the fragmented energy of habit and have no long-lasting benefit.

Substance comes from the infinite variations of habit. Through the energy of our habits, we do not notice that any substance that comes into existence is already perishing, and that all substance is continually beginning and ending within each instant, throughout infinite instants, whether these instants are conceived of as short or long. That is why there are always only instant situations within duality. With the materialist view, we can only arrive at instant conclusions based on dualistic concepts.

Even if we think that a fundamental and ultimate constituent of substance can be found, nothing can be found by finding. By being found, the pure fundamental nature of original mind automatically escapes, so whatever is found will never be the source of phenomena. It will just be an additional concept that comes and goes. The nature of delusion is to instantly appear and instantly disappear in this way.

Phenomena are just the miraculous, flirtatious show of mind. Since mind cannot stop, we uselessly cause infinite, self-deceiving phenomena by continuously remaining in duality, creating dualistic projections of worldly phenomena such as philosophy, art, and science. Then we create theories about these dualistic projections, which in time we think of as facts until they are disproven by new theories, which in turn become new facts that are again disproven by new theories. We perpetually examine whether or not new theories are true, although these objects of examination are only temporarily arising interdependent appearances that will not remain.

If we always rely on instant circumstances with the aim of finding tangible explanations of phenomena, we will ultimately only find negligible aspects of substance. All substance that arises has the seed of dissolution, so everything found by dualistic mind, which is inevitably substance, will always fluctuate back and forth and cause hope and frustration. We may give names to the phenomena of the universe and space, but these will only be the conceptual dust of mind's fundamental particle universe and the obscured space of dualistic mind. It is as if one speck of dust is found in the immeasurable expanse of phenomena and then identified as the basis of phenomena. Even what we cannot find or explain will become substantial if we conceptualize it, so even nonsubstance can be born through naming it. Mind's illusions then arise between the ideas of substance and nonsubstance, causing delusion and sa.msāra. Whether mind creates conceptions of an inner subject or an outer object, it is deluded. Whether the object of deluded mind is momentarily unpleasant or pleasant, it is still a hallucination. As one scholar said:

> When the magic city of delusion disappears into empty desert.
> The eyes again find an illusory jewel.

It is a mistake to confuse the theories of modern physics with Buddhist theories of emptiness and phenomena. Even if an idea of emptiness as the vacuous absence of phenomena is accepted by nonspiritual scientists, the great, empty space of their own limitless mind, which is the sky of wisdom, is not acknowledged. Scientific theories of relative phenomena are totally different from the Hīnayāna and Mahāyāna Buddhist teachings on the interdependence of phenomena. The result of nonspiritual scientific theory is the creation of substantial phenomena. The intention of Buddhism is to create substanceless light phenomena. Also, no parallel can be made between nonspiritual scientific explanations of phenomena, which come from dualistic mind, and the Vajrayāna Buddhist teachings of the clear appearance of nonsubstantial appearance, which come from wisdom mind. From the point of view of nihilist science, fundamental, original mind is completely ignored as the source of phenomena, and no connection is even considered between phenomena and wisdom mind.

If we examine objective phenomena, we will find that its source is subjective ego. If we examine subjective ego, we will find that the source of objective phenomena does not exist because the subject does not exist as a substantial reality. If we can recognize that phenomena never come to us, but only from us, the blossoming of fundamental inner pure Buddha phenomena becomes indistinguishable from outer pure Buddha phenomena, through practice. Then, all phenomena can be transformed into the appearance of enlightenment, abiding in the awareness of immeasurable, indivisible, nongrasping phenomena.

Whenever a fundamental, imperceptible particle of phenomena is pursued by nonspiritual science to find the source of phenomena, or even if an ultimate attribute of mind is pursued with grasping in spiritual practice, it eventually results in the maniacal frenzy of this world.

The followers of the Vaibhāṣika doctrine of Hīnayāna Buddhism examine the fundamental particle only to eradicate ego with the serenity of samādhi. Their point of view in considering objective phenomena is to realize detachment of the individual mind from phenomena in order to be liberated through realization of egoless wisdom mind to attain self-benefitting peace, which is the Hīnayāna stage of enlightenment.

According to this doctrine, fundamental, indivisible mind is absolute truth. The fundamental, indivisible particle of phenomena existing independently of mind is the ultimate source of objective phenomena and relative truth. All of the immeasurable phenomena of saṃsāra must have an origin, so the relatively existing fundamental object of general phenomena is not denied even if one's own personal goal is to reach enlightenment. But there is also no reason to examine it further, because it only exists according to relative truth for the explanation of general phenomena and as the basis of karma.

The Vaibhāṣika doctrine teaches that the practitioner can individually establish the egolessness of self by recognizing that it has no personal existence. By abstaining from the desirable objects of saṃsāra, by purifying the ego, which is the source of the passions, and by meditating, enlightenment can be attained.

According to the Mahāyāna, if the fundamental origin of phenomena exists as an indivisible particle, as the Vaibhāṣika doctrine says, then it cannot logically be compounded to result in interdependent phenomena because it is fundamental and singular. If this particle is compounded, then it is no longer fundamental and indivisible. A fundamental particle is just a concept of substance. Still, the Mahāyāna doctrine acknowledges the Vaibhāṣika doctrine's point of view as Buddha's teachings and as a skillful method within relative truth, reflecting individual capacities in order to gradually connect beings' minds to full enlightenment.

The point of view of the Mādhyamika doctrine of Mahāyāna recognizes both the egolessness of self and the sourcelessness of phenomena. Both one's personal ego and all general phenomena are equally illusory and come from interdependent circumstances, having no real existence. They are just empty forms appearing like magic as the mind's projections from countless, previous lives' habits of duality. So the main root of the path, according to the Mahāyāna, is to purify any contradictory, dualistic, substance habit which is the continual cause of saṃsāra and to realize nonsubstantial wisdom space. So, therefore, it is said as a prayer to attain that state:

> Within one particle, there are immeasurable Buddhafields,
> And in them are all inconceivable Buddhas,
> Abiding in the center of Bodhisattvas.
> Look at this to attain the activity of enlightenment.

According to the Vajrayāna revelation of the source of appearance of measureless wisdom maṇḍala, the unobstructed creation of phenomena manifests from wisdom awareness. These phenomena are used with faith and practice in order to expand immeasurable, natural, positive phenomena and to abide in that state. Unobstructedness means that the uncompounded emanation of immeasurable qualities is always open for anything at any time because nothing remains in any one limited, particular quality or within any one time. That is why there are inevitably and always the Triple Gems of the Buddha, Dharma, and Sangha according to the tradition of general Buddhism, and all wisdom deities whose essence is the same as the Triple Gems according to the tradition of Vajrayāna.

The main point of view is that from the beginningless beginning, the fundamental source of phenomena is timeless and limitless because unobstructed wisdom mind is beginninglessly vast and measurelessly expansive. By recognizing that everything can always appear, anything can manifest as wisdom deity and pureland.

The immeasurable, pure expanse of spacious wisdom sky is the origin of all elements of phenomena. Without the space of sky, nothing can appear because nothing can happen without space. Sky space is everywhere. Even according to the relative truth of ordinary beings, without sky space, water cannot flow, fire cannot flame, wind cannot arise, and earth cannot be firm. The most fundamental source is sky space. Sky space has no original substance, so it is not necessary to cause conceptions of original substance. Sky mind by itself is the immeasurable, open greeting. That is why it is said in the *Guhyagharba*:

> Unoriginating natural mind
> Is the origination of all phenomena.

Simple Logic

Worldly beings argue with me,
But I am not going to argue with them.

— LORD BUDDHA

The state of enlightenment is beyond any point of view, but Buddhas reveal many different points of view reflecting the many different phenomena of sentient beings who have not reached that state in order to guide us to enlightenment. Buddhist logic is used as a method to establish these points of view, with the ultimate purpose of releasing us from the tangible reality delusion of saṃsāra's suffering to Buddha's wisdom mind.

The ordinary logic of nihilism is used for reasoning within ordinary reality. This logic is based on the limited perception of ordinary awareness that results from the habit of only seeing and believing what is apparent and observable. The truth of its premises is only defined and confirmed by personal and general phenomena, which differ between beings and change between circumstances. Since what is logical to some beings in some situations is illogical to other beings in other situations, it is impossible for ordinary logic to accommodate the phenomena of all beings and always remain completely true. Since ordinary logic is limited to relative truth, it eventually becomes illogical and can never be used to reach an unequivocal conclusion.

Buddhist logic is used to reach enlightenment through believing in, proving, and attaining sublime qualities. Because Buddhists acknowledge other levels of awareness, they can develop and reason

26

with other levels of logic. As a result, Buddhist logic is not ordinary logic; it is pure, spiritual logic which shows self-evident truth.

Buddhist logic distinguishes between three levels of evidence for determining the nature of phenomena. The first level, the evidence of accurate perception by faultless senses, establishes the existence of conspicuous, observable phenomena.

The next level, the evidence of signs, establishes the existence of inconspicuous, nonobservable phenomena. For example, when we see smoke rising above a mountain, we can infer that there is a fire on the other side even though it is not visible, or when we see seagulls, we can assume that somewhere there is a sea.

The final level, the evidence of the wisdom speech of sublime beings such as the omniscient Buddha, establishes the existence of phenomena that cannot be perceived by the obscured senses of ordinary beings, when there are not any conspicuous phenomena or signs of inconspicuous phenomena.

We cannot say that something does not exist because we have not personally observed it. Although time and place limit the perceptions of ordinary beings, they do not affect the inconceivable nature of the appearance of Buddhas. As Renowned Moon, Dawa Drakpa, has said:

> Whoever has unclear vision
> Cannot affect those with clear vision.
> Whoever deserts stainless wisdom mind
> Cannot affect those with stainless wisdom mind.

There are many systems in Buddhism for determining the true nature of phenomena according to the various perspectives of beings with different faculties. All of these systems can be synthesized into determining the nature of phenomena according to the two categories of conditional evidence and unconditional evidence.

Conditional evidence is the evidence of the limited knowledge of ordinary perception and shows the temporary truth of the phenomena of samsaric existence. Whatever is known by ordinary perception cannot remain true. For example, worldly laws, customs, and values always change since sentient beings' perceptions always change because of their limitations. No matter what conditional evidence is perceived and named by deluded perception, it always becomes false since it is based on a temporary understanding of the changeable conditions of relative truth reached through the judgment of fragmented, obscured senses.

Pure, unconditional evidence is the evidence of the unlimited awareness of the unobscured senses of sublime beings and shows the boundless pantology of both tangible, samsaric phenomena and intangible, nonappearing appearances. This evidence has no delusion that can obstruct natural purity. For example, sublime beings see the presence of Buddha nature within the ordinary mind of each sentient being. We must have faith in the flawless speech of sublime beings which reveals the pure, unconditional evidence of absolute truth so that we can connect to their inconceivable qualities.

In order to decide what we think is true about ordinary or spiritual phenomena, we must have the conviction of knowing what is undeceptively true through the extraordinary logic of sublime beings. If our aim is to know what is ultimately true and beneficial, we must use ordinary logic with the intention of connecting to sublime logic. The benefit of conditional evidence is only that it establishes the faults of the deluded nature of all samsaric phenomena which are created by the five skandhas or six senses so that they can be recognized. This evidence is the most enthusiastically accepted truth of beings with deluded mind, though it is ultimately untrue. The benefit of pure, unconditional evidence is that it establishes the nature of all phenomena, from the Buddha nature of the vehicle of cause up to the spontaneous maṇḍala of the Great Perfection. This evidence is the most faithfully accepted truth of the followers of actual Buddhism.

Belief in only conditional evidence will not lead us to enlightenment because it is too constricted to let us see expansively. By only depending on the ordinary, temporary truth of the moment, we cannot enter the path of sublime beings. That is why Buddha said:

> Whatever is known through the perceptions of the ordinary senses of seeing, hearing, smelling, tasting, and touching is not the ultimate truth. If the perceptions of ordinary senses were ultimately true, what benefit could the path of sublime beings have for anyone?

We cannot rely on our ordinary senses. We can only rely on sublime beings who see pure truth. Sublime beings only reflect temporary conditional evidence for sentient beings with ordinary perceptions in order to guide us to the unconditional evidence of absolute truth, which is the pure, clear phenomena of the Buddhafields of enlightenment. Enlightenment is the essence of what is most meaningful, revealed through the vast logic of many sublime beings.

In the absolute truth of the measureless appearances of the Buddhas, there is not any reason to name different categories of Dharma, because there is only the all-pervading purity of enlightenment, which is beyond conceptual categorizations. However, within relative truth, since sentient beings are limitless, the ways in which Dharma is conveyed to them are also limitless. In order to clearly analyze different points of view and to be able to choose the right point of view, Dharma teachings can be categorized as the Dharma of revealed meaning and the Dharma of realization.

The Dharma of revealed meaning is the spontaneous manifestation of Buddhas' speech within form, which comes from inconceivable wisdom mind. It can occur within any language in the universe in order to guide beings according to their capacity. When the mind receives the blessings of this wisdom speech, wisdom qualities can be recognized and opened through practice until practice is transformed into the nondualistic wisdom appearance of Buddhas. The Dharma of realization, which is the essence of the Dharma of revealed meaning, is the nondualistic wisdom appearance which is the mani-

festation of the attainment of wisdom mind. Both of these aspects of
Dharma come from the limitless, supreme wisdom Rūpakāya senses
of the Buddhas, which are inseparable from measureless, sky-wisdom
Dharmakāya.

In order to attain the Dharma of realization, those who are entering on the path must respectfully depend on the Dharma of revealed
meaning. Then they can increase pure, light wisdom through prayer
and meditation until there is no difference between the Dharma of
revealed meaning and the Dharma of realization, which is the same as
all Buddhas.

The teachings of the Buddhas are always pure and always illuminate the sole expanse of unity. The activity of the Buddhas can
only benefit since it always comes from stainless wisdom appearance.
Whatever comes from this source is the teaching of holy Dharma,
which never causes recircling in saṃsāra and always points to the ultimate purity.

The Buddhas abide in measureless pure appearances. From their
effortless, guiding wisdom speech and spontaneous manifestation of
infinite qualities, they can bring sentient beings to this state of pure
appearances through many extensive traditions or through one sim-
plest tradition of holy Dharma, which comes from the pure wisdom
heart of the Buddhas.

Cleaning Deviations

My speech is inconceivable, so no one can
  see it,
But my speech is everything, so everyone
  can understand it.

— LORD BUDDHA

In order to attain the immaculate state of Buddhafields, our habits must be purified. This can only happen if we have a point of view that acknowledges the nonsubstantial basis of mind. In the daytime, a person may wash his body clean, but at night, he can still dream he is dirty. Habits cannot be purified by substantial methods. They are purified by spiritual practice.

If we believe that mind is the source of all substantial and non-substantial appearances, we can decide that mind is limitless and believe in our own Buddha nature, which inspires us to practice. Then, by recognizing even just one clear spark of natural awareness, this spark can become the great flame that burns the jungle of dualistic habit's confusion and is the origin of the vast, luminous appearance of the immeasurable sky of enlightenment.

The teachings of Buddhism reveal that mind is the basis of the infinite variations of phenomena, encouraging us to influence our own phenomena so that we can try to create positive energy through positive intention in order to go beyond our habits and recognize natural awareness. But many people have opinions about Buddhism that are based on misunderstandings, like arrows that are shot before finding an exact target. This interferes with being able to realize the actual meaning of Buddhist teachings, allowing the contradictions of unawareness to arise.

Some people think that Buddhism is a philosophy and not a religion; but Buddhism is neither a nihilist philosophy nor an eternalist religion. This is a complete deviation whose source is material judgment, made by people who try to find out about Buddhism but merely focus on its objective, material aspects out of their own material habit. Through only paying attention to the outer appearances and activities of Buddhist organizations and scholars, they only see Buddhists studying and debating, without understanding that the purpose of their study is to lead to practice and to open wisdom. Then, deciding that what is studied and debated resembles the refined logic of some subtle, worldly philosophies, they speculate that the ultimate teaching of Buddhism must be philosophy. They do not see meditators who are practicing inconspicuously, and they do not see the development of their inconceivable, naturally secret, spiritual qualities which cannot be observed because they are intangible.

The Buddhist view is to recognize that we must not remain within ordinary phenomena by following a worldly philosophy limited to ordinary, substantial reasoning. We must decide to increase pure phenomena by following a spiritual philosophy which goes beyond ordinary reasoning and leads to enlightenment. Buddhist philosophy is entirely spiritual. Its purpose is to refute the views of the two extremes of nihilism and eternalism by the skillful means of wisdom, to release all beings to enlightenment.

Some nihilists in particular think that Buddhism is only a philosophy and not a religion. This misunderstanding is the result of holding the nihilist point of view, which does not accept the intangible, imperceptible qualities of nondualistic wisdom that can appear tangibly or intangibly. Because the nihilist point of view is confined to the reasoning of dualistic mind, it is actually impossible to use it to define or evaluate the qualities of Buddhism deeply and clearly, since they are beyond ordinary perception. Even the difference between ordinary and spiritual qualities cannot be analyzed.

If all that is noticed is what is reflected in a small mirror as though nothing else existed, many other forms and colors that can appear are not seen. Yet just as a clear ocean can reflect the light of countless stars, Buddhism can reflect any of the countless views that benefit beings, including many different philosophies, without being limited to any particular philosophy.

The pith of nihilism is disbelief in anything beyond the appearance of perceptible, material phenomena, because there is no awareness or recognition of the phenomena that are beyond the reality and perception of ordinary, obscured senses. This disbelief is not limited to modern nihilism, because nihilism has existed ever since beings have existed. The only difference between past, present, and future nihilism is in the particular way that substance is used within the circumstances of time and place.

The nihilist view of believing only in this momentary life is the result of considering substance to be the fundamental constituent of all phenomena, including one's body, the objective gross elements, whatever arises from these gross elements, and whatever can be perceived. There are many different ways to understand substance within relative truth, since there are infinite relative truths. Nihilism means becoming caught within each temporary circumstance of relative truth and believing in its reality, so the perception of substance seems real.

From the Buddhist point of view, everything that exists in saṃsāra is substance. The origin of substance is dualistic mind. There is no end to substance because there is no end to the conceptions of dualistic mind. Whenever the Buddha nature of sentient beings is dormant and dualistic mind appears, the ordinary passions and the incalculable phenomena of the karmic elements arise, which are all composed of substance.

Substance only exists within the compounded circumstances of relative truth as interdependent, relative appearances. It is not only a perceptible result; it can also be an imperceptible cause, since anything that causes substance is itself substance, such as imperceptible conceptions. Substance only comes from the root circumstance conception of a subject and the contributing circumstance of time and place in which phenomena objectively arise. Since sentient beings' minds are infinite, they create endless conceptions, which create endless substance.

Substance is not only one part of something. It is all the immeasurable forms of samsaric existence, unless it is transformed into immeasurable, substanceless, wisdom light appearances which are beyond all interdependent cause and result. This is the meaning of substancelessness. Substanceless wisdom is unobstructed and pervades everywhere in saṃsāra and nirvāṇa without intention as self-accomplished compassion, so it can manifest within substance, but it never remains there. Its essence is always nonsubstance, which is the quality of Buddha.

Substancelessness can be realized from different points of view within Buddhism in order to transcend nihilism. The followers of Hīnayāna Buddhism believe in detachment from substance through the realization of selflessness. The followers of Mahāyāna Buddhism believe that any appearance of substance is only habit and has no actual ground, like the moon's image mirrored in water; it is only the illusory reflection of mind, and mind does not exist because it is beyond fabrication. The followers of Vajrayāna Buddhism believe that ordinary substance is naturally stainless, so whatever occurs is actually pure appearance, and whatever is pure appearance is deity.

Some nihilists think that there are correspondences between nihilist and Buddhist ideas, comparing them in order to show that they are ultimately the same. But no matter how many temporary similarities seem to be found between them, nihilist ideas are always connected either directly or indirectly to tangible, material qualities, and Buddhist ideas are always connected either directly or indirectly to intangible, spiritual qualities. Buddhism only uses tangible, material ideas and the impermanent phenomena of substance peripherally, as a support for making the connection to their intangible essence. Also, nihilism and Buddhism always have a different aim. The nihilist aim never goes beyond the limitation of its own momentary ideas of substance. The Buddhist aim is to increase substanceless wisdom qualities, which are the unchangeable ecstasy of peace. In Buddhism, the basis of the point of view, the path of practice, and the result of the activity always connect to inconceivable enlightenment.

While nihilists view relative truth as the fixed, factual existence of a definite reality, Buddhists view relative truth as the versatile, temporary result of different beings' personal and general phenomena. Because all phenomena are filtered through our subjectivity, Buddhists believe that both subject and object are fooling us, and that all phenomena including ourselves are actually egoless.

Nihilists never believe that consciousness and circumstances arise through karma created by habits planted in ālaya, the basis of mind. They think that consciousness is completely dependent on substance, and that when death occurs and the circumstances of substance vanish, mind also vanishes. Although this acknowledges a connection between substance and mind, the connection is only made through substance. By thinking that mind exists only because of substantial phenomena, it is not recognized that substantial phenomena only exist because of mind.

Some eternalists think that Buddhism is a form of nihilism. This is often because they believe that Buddhism has no god, which means they think Buddhists do not depend on the same gods or follow the same theistic traditions as eternalists do. Also, it should be noticed that some people who seem to be eternalists may actually have a point of view that is close to nihilism without being aware of it, if their beliefs originate from and depend on substantial ideas. They may only follow eternalist traditions without actually connecting their own minds with these beliefs. In this way, their beliefs can only be an outer, substantial facade and like any other nihilist delusion of reality. Although spiritual appearances can occur both within form and formlessly, spiritual qualities cannot be recognized by only accepting the forms of eternalist traditions, gods, and beliefs with a material point of view.

Also, some eternalists think that Buddhism is a form of nihilism because they completely misunderstand the meaning of the Buddhist view of great emptiness, and particularly the view of great emptiness in the Mādhyamika teachings. The Buddhist view of emptiness is misinterpreted as being a vacuous, nihilistic nothingness which is a negation of all phenomena and an inert absence of gods. This misinterpretation is made through a lack of thorough study of the Mahāyāna point of view as Buddha Śakyamuni revealed it, and which many sublime teachers, including Nāgārjuna, have explained.

In the Mahāyāna teachings, according to the basis, the selfless point of view of the selflessness of the personal ego and the selflessness of phenomena are established as free from mental activity in order to not grasp at phenomena or cause samsaric seeds. But until dualistic mind vanishes into one's own unending awareness mind through meditation, immeasurable, inconceivable, enlightened Buddhas still exist objectively as reflections of subjective Buddha nature. Therefore, according to the path, without remaining in nothingness, the practice of the ocean of the accumulation of merit and wisdom is accomplished, the ocean of samsaric sentient beings is ripened into the fruit of enlightenment, and the ocean of purelands is attained, in order to unite subjective Buddha nature and objective Buddhas, which becomes the immeasurable quality of enlightenment. According to the result, the objective existence of all immeasurable, inconceivable, enlightened Buddhas is united with subjective Buddha nature, which becomes the oneness of immeasurable, inconceivable, enlightened Buddha phenomena always. These inconceivable Buddhas are always beyond both the nihilist void and all the gods of the eternalist imagination.

The great, stainless emptiness of space, which is Dharmakāya, is inseparable with Rūpakāya, which is the pure phenomena of Sambhogakāya and Nirmānakāya. Since the quality of Dharmakāya is always stainless, it never falls to the substantialism of eternalist gods. Also, since it is stainless, it is naturally unobstructed and indivisible from the infallible, unending, inconceivable manifestations of Rūpakāya. So therefore, it never falls to the nothingness of nihilism. This shows that a negation of phenomena does not exist within the basis, path, or result of Mahāyāna. The meaning of this is freedom forever from the two extremes of nihilism and eternalism, which is the Dharmakāya body of appearance.

The compassion of Buddhas, which is the spontaneous appearance of the great emptiness of Dharmakāya enlightenment, is proof that Buddhism is not nihilistic. Buddhas benefit sentient beings continuously and unceasingly as a result of the accumulation of prayers and aspirations made for sentient beings by Bodhisattvas before they attained Buddhahood. Even when Buddhas are enlightened, this benefit is continuous, though for Buddhas, there is no object of sentient beings to be benefitted or subject who benefits. Buddhas have no dualistic intention to grant the wishes of beings, yet effortless benefit occurs, like the precious jewels that spontaneously appear on a wish-fulfilling tree. All Buddhas' teachings are the intentionless revelation of unobstructed wisdom resonance, so there is not any way to misinterpret Buddhism as nihilism.

Some people think that Buddhism is a form of eternalism. Through their misunderstanding, they do not realize that when Buddhists worship, pray, and offer to any of the supreme aspects of Buddhas or their tangible and intangible images, it is not with an eternalist point of view.

The pith of the general eternalist point of view is that gods and heavens have a permanent existence which is distinct from personal phenomena. The gods which eternalists believe in are turned into objects, whether these gods are considered to exist with form, without form, as a single god, or as many gods. This is because the essential nature of mind is separated from the essential nature of deity. Although the eternalist point of view may seem to connect worshipers with their gods, these gods are not recognized as reflections of mind. Because eternalists do not have the point of view that Buddha nature is inherent within us, they always relate to their gods as originally existing independently of their own mind. The Buddhist aim is to go beyond this duality by transforming the separation of self from other into indivisible deity, which is enlightenment. Buddhists believe that deity only arises as the result of one's own pure perception, and it is only through this recognition that dualistic mind is surpassed.

Even within Buddhism, some followers of the Hīnayāna teachings think that Mahāyāna Buddhism is eternalist because of their misunderstanding of the Mahāyāna teachings on the certainty of always manifesting, luminous Sambhogakāya appearance. However, the quality of the Mahāyāna certainty of always manifesting is not eternalist because this manifestation is only self-appearance that is never separated from great emptiness. It is the natural, radiant clarity of space, free from the reality of any enduring, objective gods. It is never concretized into objective permanence.

From the Mahāyāna Buddhist point of view, each sentient being has the potential of Buddha nature from the beginning, so the aim is to practice in order to awaken the awareness of one's inseparability from this inherent nature. From the high Vajrayāna Buddhist point of view, no one has ever been separated from all Buddhas. That is why Vajrayāna practice uses the result of the maṇḍalas of Buddhas even as the path. Pure Buddha is never separate from the appearance of natural awareness, which is beyond duality. But as long as Buddhists have dualistic phenomena, they worship deity objectively in order to purify this duality by transforming ordinary conceptions of subject and object into noncontradictory Buddha phenomena. As a result of practice which purifies obscurations and increases confidence, Buddhists believe they can become one with deity and pureland.

In this substantial world, when a person who lives on one continent cannot see other continents, it does not mean that other continents do not exist. In the same way, Buddhists believe that the immeasurable purelands of mind's reflections exist even if, from lack of recognition and faith, they do not see them due to the ocean of their karmic obscurations. It is not possible to recognize purelands without recognizing the origin of divine reflection, which is each individual's wisdom mind. So, Buddhists practice in order to purify ordinary perception and see what is naturally there.

According to the teachings of many wise scholars and saints, deities and their purelands may seem to exist apart from us as long as we rely on relative truth. However, this does not mean that we must travel with our karmic bodies to reach them. As long as there is dualistic mind, we are unavoidably involved with either the tangible or intangible objects of our imagination. So therefore, even if we consider ourselves to be Buddhists, we cannot impetuously and unfaithfully ignore or disrespect positive objects until we have transcended the division of subject and object.

When we are inseparable from pureland and the pureland's deity, there is no discrimination between whether the deity and pureland have come to us or we have gone to them. No distinction is made between external and internal existence, because dualistic habit has vanished into indestructible oneness and everything is inseparable. This is not like human thinking that separates outer elements and inner beings. Pureland is wisdom mind, and wisdom mind is pureland. The deity's palace is deity, and deity is the deity's palace. This inseparability is called the great unity.

According to the path of enlightenment, when Buddhists accumulate merit by visualizing and worshiping supreme wisdom deity Buddhas objectively, they purify all samsaric perceptions by not continuously remaining in the ordinary subject of their ego's habit, which is the cause of suffering. Then, gradually, inseparability with wisdom deity is attained in the unobscured, great space of the immeasurable offering of self-manifesting. Just like one's reflection coming back to oneself from a stainless mirror, the one who offers, the one who accepts the offering, and the offering itself are not different. That is why it is said that wisdom is the display of wisdom.

In order to recognize this and to let our Buddha nature blossom, we must have faith in all Buddhas and sublime beings who exist everywhere until Buddha nature becomes the indivisible expanse of full enlightenment. If we do not have faith in outer Buddhas, it is a sign of not believing in our own Buddha nature. As long as we do not believe in our own Buddha nature, ordinary mind's projections of demons and gods will occur and we will think that they have a separate, objective reality.

If people sometimes have objective circumstances with negative energy which they name as particular supernatural demons from their own negative habit of projection over many lives, they build reflections of negative energy. They feel these demons are harming them and try to stop them, escape from them, or exorcise them. Through not recognizing Buddha nature, they do not see that these demons are created by their own mind and reflecting back to them.

If they sometimes have objective circumstances with positive energy which they name as particular supernatural gods and goddesses from their own positive habit of projection of many lives, they build reflections of positive energy. They feel these gods and goddesses are benefitting them and try to imagine them, see them, or worship them. Through not recognizing Buddha nature, they do not see that these gods and goddesses are created by their own mind and reflecting back to them.

Then, whenever the negativity created over many lives returns to those who believe in eternalist gods, they think that their gods have betrayed them, and they betray their gods. They worship gods in order to receive positive circumstances and phenomena, thinking that this will make them prosper in this life and that they can go to heaven after this life. But if suddenly negative circumstances occur such as illness, war, disasters, or whatever causes them to be miserable, they do not realize that these circumstances are karmic results they have created from their own dualistic habit over many lives. This mistake is made by those who do not believe in Buddha nature or have faith in enlightenment. Out of ignorance about the karmic system and lack of recognition that all phenomena are created by mind, they are always looking outwardly.

Since these people cannot explain their negative circumstances, they think that their gods have created what they have themselves created. So, believing their gods are bad for causing negativity, they abandon them. The crux of this mistake, although it is made by eternalists, is actually the nihilist habit of wanting immediate, substantial rewards. This always causes self-destruction.

According to Buddhism, negativity is not created by gods. Even if people are ready to abandon their gods when negative circumstances arise, they cannot actually do this unless dualistic mind is abandoned, just as they cannot abandon their shadow unless they abandon their body. They blame gods because they believe gods are creators. Yet the thought that gods are creators comes from the creator which is one's own mind. These people think that the object creator betrayed the subject creator, because they think their gods have created them and their circumstances and then have tortured and punished them. But abandoning god is only the subject creator betraying the object creator. There is no proof of who has betrayed whom, and these people just continuously circle between betrayals with nihilist and eternalist habits that lead to each other with ominous monotony.

Buddhism does not cause betrayal between subject and object, but teaches how to go beyond subject and object through using refluent, positive energy and positive phenomena to attain enlightenment.

Those who have faith in Mahāyāna Buddhism are supposed to believe totally in the Buddha nature of each sentient being and believe that all nihilists and eternalists have the potential to be enlightened. The only problem for sentient beings is their insistence on renewing their samsaric insurance of keeping and choosing nihilist and eternalist habits over many lives and not believing in Buddha nature.

From the Buddhist point of view, there is no separate, independent existence of nihilists or eternalists, because Buddha nature pervades each sentient being's mind. Whoever has mind, including nihilists and eternalists, has Buddha nature, and can become enlightened the same as Buddha. Nihilism and eternalism are just aspects of mind, created by dualistic misinterpretations. Even though nihilists and eternalists do not accept the potential of Buddha nature, there is no question that at some time they can eventually realize it through the root circumstance of their Buddha nature meeting the contributing circumstance of Buddha's teachings.

The habits of nihilism and eternalism are only momentary vascillations of mind. When one habit is dormant, another habit is conspicuous, just as when river water rises, fewer stones are seen, and when it falls, more stones appear. Within one single mind, sometimes the habit of nihilism is apparent, and sometimes the habit of eternalism is apparent, but the essence of each sentient being's mind is Buddha nature. Actually, all nihilism and eternalism are the same as Buddhism if they self-correct and open to become as they are. It is only through mind's misinterpretation that the habit of a different point of view is formed and a position is taken that is named nihilism or eternalism. Other than that, different realms of nihilism and eternalism do not exist. So, in order not to waste our minds with saṃsāra's static, we must believe in Buddhism's sublime teachings until reaching self-correcting confidence, in order to attain enlightenment for the benefit of all sentient beings.

Some scholars think that only Hīnayāna Dharma is genuine Buddhism. Either they doubt the validity of Mahāyāna and Vajrayāna Dharma, or they think they are eternalist. Through their pedantic interpretations of certain texts, these scholars think they have the historical proof to determine which teachings are authentic. But their intellectual substantiation does not prove anything. It only further obscures their Buddha nature so that they do not see the vast, unfathomable nature of the omniscient Buddhas' teachings and they lose their connection to the infallible essence of Buddhism. The main point of Buddhism can be missed through the nihilist habit of having fixed, intellectual ideas, hastily looking in particular texts for material answers to questions about immaterial sublime qualities, and not looking at the nature of mind. Buddhism cannot be defined or understood by mere bookish verbiage. It is necessary to establish a profound point of view with faith, blessings, wisdom teachings, and the practice of samādhi in order to be able to fathom the vast meaning of Buddhism.

Some people think that only Hīnayāna Buddhist texts written in Sanskrit are authentic Buddhist teachings. They believe that they are distilling Buddhism with great respect by only accepting teachings of Buddha that can be validated with the historical, material evidence of certain Sanskrit texts. But this position is actually disrespectful. Through basic ignorance of the inconceivable qualities of Buddhas' teachings, it denigrates Buddha's speech and misleads others by mistakenly interpolating its view. By trying to limit Buddha's boundless teaching to a particular form that can be confirmed by material evidence according to ordinary, general phenomena, it rejects other expansive aspects that benefit beings with keen faculties. Holding this view is contradictory even from its own perspective, and is an indication of not believing in the omniscience of the Buddhas who can reveal limitless teachings.

Even though these people may not have had the fortunate karma to have met with the Mahāyāna and Vajrayāna teachings, there are Mahāyāna and Vajrayāna texts which are written in Sanskrit, as well as in Pali and other languages. Of course, Sanskrit is a precious language since Buddha Śakyamuni taught in Sanskrit. However, Sanskrit has not only been used for writing about Dharma, and other languages can also be used by sentient beings to connect with Buddha's blessings. For instance, many sublime beings have translated Dharma into Tibetan according to the meaning, so that the Tibetan language has had a unique development of Buddhist terms. From the blessings of these sublime beings, Tibetan Dharma words are full of essence.

Buddha says in the sutras that his reflection corresponds to sentient beings' time, place, and faculties, so this cannot mean only one reflection concocted by a rigid mind. Buddha has unobstructed wisdom speech. As it is written in the sūtras:

43

I will teach with the sounds of gods, with the sounds of nāgas, with the sounds of yakshas, with the sounds of gandharvas, and with the sounds of human beings. However many sounds of sentient beings exist, with that many sounds I will teach.

Also, from *The Sūtra of Stainless Light*:

> Without knowing the sounds of all sentient beings,
> Only teaching from the one minor aspect of the sound
>   of Sanskrit,
> Then Buddha will be made small.

Some people think only one tradition of Buddhism is right and other traditions are wrong. This kind of sectarianism, which deprecates other Buddhist traditions, shows that wisdom has not been realized. If mind is not used to create wisdom, strong dualistic ego obsessively rejects and accepts, causing hatred toward others who are different and attachment to one's own way, which is the basis of sectarianism. Of course, it is good to have loyalty and faith in one's own tradition, but only without devaluing and having hatred toward other traditions that are suitable for those with different phenomena.

Sectarianism is based on the false pride of dualistic ego's delusion of superiority. It is uninfluenced by wisdom blessings. When sectarians take a position, they build enormous arrogance. Even if they do not say so, they think their own view is the best and they are condescending to others. It is very dangerous for them to teach, because their students copy them and many generations can follow their wrong point of view. This only causes negative energy and creates tautological arguments for the purpose of honoring self-righteous ego.

Although sectarians may seem to be studying spiritual teachings, they are only disguising dualistic mind's ruminations with a spiritual veneer. The reason for studying spiritual teachings is to subdue ordinary ego and open wisdom mind. No matter what traditions are studied, the purpose of study is to go beyond sectarian views. When wisdom mind opens, there is automatically a total loss of interest in outward, intellectual study and sectarianism, since the immeasurable knowledge of wisdom opens from the treasure of wisdom mind. If wisdom mind opens without studying, the meaning of studying is still achieved, which is the manifestation of wisdom Buddha. Abiding in wisdom mind is nonsectarianism.

Some people study Dharma without thoroughly learning about its many different perspectives, but just sniffing them and glancing at what they look like. Although they do not understand even one tradition's perspective deeply and clearly, they use vainglorious expressions of nonsectarianism. Then, through their melting pot habit, they mix up the uncomplementary ideas they have collected from various sources. Instead of creating a pristine river that soothes and nourishes their minds by giving positive phenomena, they make a filthy cesspool of confusion and sit in it for their whole lives, thinking it is the state of nonsectarianism.

In general, it is difficult to judge who is sectarian and who is nonsectarian. For example, some people who are actually nonsectarian may seem to be sectarian because they do not associate with many people from other traditions in many sophisticated spiritual activities. But this may be because they are predominantly focusing inwardly, trying to nourish what they know through their own teaching's tradition in order to open nondualistic wisdom, rather than outwardly trying to look good in front of others. They do not care what other people will say or think about them, even if they are accused of being sectarian, because they do not want to trick themselves and others by making a show of being nonsectarian.

Many people think and say that everyone is supposed to be open, but though the doors of their mouths are open, the gates of their minds are tightly closed with their rusty, iron ego's latch. This pseudo-nonsectarian attitude actually feeds ego. Often these people only want to use Dharma ideas for building self-aggrandizing positions rather than for enlightenment. Yet a sign of nonsectarianism is not holding any position of this or that. Even though these people call themselves nonsectarian, they try to support their own position by intellectualizing their misunderstanding, institutionalizing their desires and beliefs, reducing sublime qualities to ordinary, marketable art, and using Dharma as capital.

There are many kinds of nonsectarian facades, but most of them can be included within three categories. One category is actually made up of sectarians who use the technique of showing a nonsectarian face through their facility with efficient Dharma politics. This is done to attract and seduce many people who have melting pot complacency without threatening them. Their purpose is to manipulate others and strengthen their own sect's material power. This deceit is dangerous for pure, naive people who truly wish to be nonsectarian, because it makes it difficult to recognize the sectarian views that exist behind what is shown. The intention of this kind of nonsectarianism is no different than that of an ambitious, political party within a multiparty coalition government that tricks people with an outward show of unity while actually only temporarily collaborating with other parties to build material power for its own interests.

The second category of nonsectarian facades is based on the indifference of nihilism, and consists of those who do not believe in or care about either the point of view of enlightenment with faith or following any particular doctrine's tradition with respect. They just use religious ideas for whatever will be beneficial in their present life. This is the same as running a business, with Dharma purchased and sold as a cultural commodity for temporary, worldly gain.

The third category is based on the dullness of indifferent stupor. It comprises people who think it is wonderful to accept all spiritual traditions but do not benefit from any of them due to a lack of commitment to practice any tradition. This is like a baby who tries to grab many stars at night but cannot get even one.

One can become actually nonsectarian by studying many doctrines with many wise teachers, truly absorbing their teachings, subduing one's ego, increasing impartiality through practice, and staying in the even noncontradiction of wisdom mind. One can also become nonsectarian without apparently studying many doctrines with many teachers if one has a gifted mind and tremendous devotion as a result of the accumulation of merit from previous lives. Then, in this life, one can become directly introduced to wisdom mind by wisdom teachers through the teachings of upadeśa. By seeing nondualistic wisdom mind through prayer, practice, and meditation, one can become genuinely nonsectarian, as previous sublime beings have done, without remaining in the biases of conceptualization.

Nonsectarianism is based on the intention to attain enlightenment by recognizing, developing, and always abiding in nondualistic wisdom with the blessing of wisdom teachers. This means that the distortions and imbalances of attachment and aversion to different points of view and doctrines have been purified. This includes the purification of the previous habit of substantial theories which cause dualistic conception and suffering, but are disguised as spiritual phenomena. Wisdom does not have any doctrine because it does not have any dualistic point of view. This is equanimity, so that is why it is nonsectarian.

Wisdom teachers are always abiding in nondualistic wisdom mind, so they are truly nonsectarian. They do not see any divisions of lower and higher qualities in Dharma phenomena since they recognize that all phenomena are one's own unobstructed manifestation and equally immaculate. Even though differentiated aspects of Dharma arise, they are all seen equally as the qualities of discerning wisdom. Instead of creating objects of discrimination with the mire of material ideas, all phenomena become the crystalline ornament of their own mind. They know that there is no reason to disturb their own mind with the stain of sectarianism by misusing Dharma to cause nonvirtue, so they have no desire to influence others to be sectarian.

Nonsectarian wisdom teachers always see purity since their minds are unstained by the contradictions of intellectual selection. Through the openness of wisdom, they see countless aspects of knowledge as expressions of one essence. Therefore, they can guide other beings according to their wishes and capacities through different traditions toward the ultimate goal of enlightenment, just as hundreds of rivers and streams flow into the same vast ocean.

Some people only want to believe in sublime beings who have manifested in perceptible, historical form in this world's reality. But by only believing in perceptible forms of sublime beings, who can appear in both perceptible form and as imperceptible energy, one is not having faith in the inexpressible qualities of the Buddhas which are the characteristics of enlightenment, beyond the habit of substantial reality's form. If we only accept the existence of what can be accommodated within our ordinary delusion, it is impossible to have faith in enlightenment, which is the infallible, pure phenomena of any Buddha and is beyond our ordinary reality.

Some people use differences between the historical accounts of particular sublime beings to dispute the truth of their existence. But before making any judgments only through historical evidence with the rigidity of a narrow mind and without any special insight, it must be remembered that even the various histories of Buddha Śakyamuni differ from each other and can be understood in many ways. For example, there are different versions within the Hīnayāna and Mahāyāna traditions of Buddha's birth, life, and turning of the wheel of Dharma. These variations are reflections of the particular faculties of sentient beings and their different capacities for understanding.

Because sublime beings are miraculous, their histories do not fit within nonspiritual reality and ordinary, intellectual reasoning. If some people cannot accept these histories because they seem inconsistent and illogical, then they cannot logically accept any of the wonderful histories of the thousand Buddhas, including Buddha Śakyamuni, as well as those of all ancient, sublime scholars, the mahāsiddhas, and even one's own guru. The histories of sublime beings can never be confined within saṃsāra's boundaries because enlightenment can never fit into ordinary mind and its ordinary calculations.

In order to open one's own wisdom mind, Buddhas must be recognized as sublime. Buddha means the unobscured expanse of wisdom qualities, which reveals how one's own mind is the source of inexhaustible qualities and immeasurable emanations of Buddhas.

Instead of creating doubt about any Buddhas, one must have faith and believe as Buddha Śakyamuni said:

> For whoever thinks of Buddha,
> Buddha is sitting in front of him,
> Always bestowing blessings
> And removing all obscurations.

Some people think that Buddhas only manifest in particular forms. But sublime beings cannot be said to always have a certain form since they can appear in any form and their emanations are miraculously unobstructed. If we expect the qualities of sublime beings to correspond to the rules of our preconceptions of reality, then we can never transfigure our nihilist habits to the glory of victorious omniscience.

When we are on the path of enlightenment, we cannot even decide how to categorize the various forms in which sublime beings manifest. For example, in general phenomena, Buddha Śakyamuni has the aspect of a self-ordained monk. But when he taught King Indrabodhi, he transformed into the maṇḍala of Guhyasamāja, in accordance with the king's keen faculties. In that aspect, Buddha is not different from Vajradhāra and does not hold the definite form of a monk. Also, Padmasambhava manifested as a monk and a wisdom scholar as well as in the aspect of a supreme vajramaster. Likewise, Sarahapa, Nāgārjuna, and many of the other eighty-four mahāsiddhas who accomplished the state of enlightenment manifested without the restriction of any specific aspect.

The eighty-four mahāsiddhas refer to those who attended a ganacakra offered by the saint Vajrasana, and the one thousand Buddhas are counted from those Bodhisattvas who met and prayed together to attain Buddhahood, as told in *The Sūtra of the Noble Eon*. Yet there are many more Buddhas and saints than those who are in these two great gatherings. Since Buddhas' manifestations are unobstructed and the Buddha nature of countless sentient beings is ready to open, countless saints and Buddhas have appeared in the past and will appear in the future, according to Buddha's teachings.

Buddhas never remain in any one place locked in a particular form, because they do not have karmic bodies, but only the unobscured light body of enlightenment, which is unable to be limited to a certain, conceptual, ordinary life history. This inspires us to practice to attain that same state.

It is not wise to be influenced by ordinary ideas about the aspect of a sublime being. For example, it is foolish to only think of Buddha Śākyamuni as a Nepalese citizen because he was born in Lumbini, instead of believing that he appeared in Nirmāṇakāya form as an unobstructed manifestation of imperceptible Dharmakāya. Enlightenment is not limited to any certain country, certain form, or certain time. As Buddha said:

> Since there is no grasping mind,
> There are no different places in Buddha's phenomena.

From ancient times until now, even sentient beings in this world have not had a certain form, so it is preposterous to think that Buddhas should be more limited than sentient beings in their manifestations. Many of the eighty-four mahāsiddhas may have appeared to have come from a specific place or time or to have manifested in a specific form, but their view was vast beyond conception and not part of a location or convention of any constricted, worldly culture. Buddhas can appear from formless, infallible Dharmakāya in any form that will benefit others, including nonhuman and human forms, with the quality of infallibility. Therefore, it is not right to try to reduce them to one's own conception of a certain, fallible form.

Thinking that Buddhas should manifest in a particular aspect is illogical, even if it is only considered according to the evidence of one's own phenomena. Since it is said many times in Buddha's teachings that all immeasurable phenomena are one's own immeasurable appearances, how can any Buddha be excluded from this infinity of possibilities? Since anything can exist, disputing the existence of any particular manifestation of the Buddhas is a sign of not even recognizing that one's own phenomena are unobstructed. Since there is always positive Buddha nature, it is not necessary to suppress it and become dispirited. Buddhas, through compassion, try to illuminate sentient beings' Buddha nature. When one's naturally unobstructed phenomena are blocked for many lives by the darkness of ignorance, light cannot be seen, and without clear insight, one decides too quickly what to believe. But anyone who has a human being's mind must recognize that one cannot stop even one's own phenomena. As the great saint Sarahapa sang:

> The sole essential nature of mind is the source of all
>   phenomena.
> Wherever existence and enlightenment manifest,
> The fruit of whatever is wished is given.
> I bow to mind, which is the wish-fulfilling jewel.

Careful examination shows that there is nothing that exists even in ordinary reality that is agreeable to everyone. There is not even a god that is acceptable to everyone. Likewise, within Buddhism, different teachings are suitable to different individual phenomena and capacities. If we believe in Buddha nature, there is no reason to discourage others from having different Buddha phenomena than one's own. Instead of using the limited, substantial logic of the habit of worldly reality to argue against particular aspects of Buddhas, we had better let Buddha nature self-manifest. The imposition of negative conceptions only further obscures one's own Buddha nature, which has already been dormant for many lives.

If one does not accept that the manifestations of Buddhas are infinite, it shows that one has not recognized the unobstructed qualities of one's own Buddha nature. According to both the doctrine of cause and the doctrine of result in the Mahāyāna tradition, all Buddhas can manifest from one's own Buddha nature.

It is very important to acknowledge the Buddha nature of one's own mind and to let it illuminate appearance freely with faith through pure phenomena. If we only judge what appears to us outwardly, without introspection, it will not even matter if we are living with all Buddhas, since we will not see their qualities because of our own impure perception. Devadatta stayed with Buddha Śakyamuni for many years, but due to jealousy, he only projected his own negativity instead of seeing Buddha's awesome qualities.

If someone defines a specific form in which Buddhas should appear, it means that they do not comprehend the three kāyas, and especially not the quality of Nirmānakāya, which appears in any miraculous form that can guide beings. Wisdom teachers in Nirmānakāya can assume any aspect that corresponds to the time, place, and capacity of beings, even though, according to absolute truth, Buddhas are beyond all times and places and hold the power of inconceivable wisdom qualities. Nirmānakāya is the miraculous uncertainty of time, place, and aspect, which is wisdom's magic appearance.

Instead of discouraging others from believing in their Buddha nature, we must encourage the blossoming of Buddha nature for ourselves and others. No matter how Buddhas appear, those who know the true meaning of Buddhist history will acknowledge that there are infinite aspects of the Nirmānakāya manifestations of Buddhas. For example, there is no need to see a contradiction between believing that Maitreya has appeared in Bodhisattva form at Buddha Śakyamuni's time and believing that Maitreya is in Tuṣita Heaven and will manifest in Buddha's form after this degenerate age has ended to be enlightened under the bodhi tree, in order to guide beings in the coming golden age.

Some people, through their obscurations, create confusion and negative conceptions by trying to differentiate between Buddhas and deities. They think either that Buddhas are better or that deities are better, and they tell others which Buddhas or deities one should believe in and which should not be believed in, according to what they themselves believe or do not believe. Of course, each person can choose his own individual aspect of Buddhas and deities. But it is not appropriate for ordinary beings to try to influence others about what they should and should not believe by substantializing Buddhas, because everyone has his own previous karmic connection with Buddhas and deities, which can only be introduced by sublime teachers.

According to the teachings of Mahāyāna Buddhism, everyone must reach enlightenment, and not just a few people in some particular group who think in the same way. Therefore, the aspects of the Buddhas are not limited to a single individual's restricted concept. Especially if someone wants to attain enlightenment, it is important not to make any material limitation of Buddhas, because Buddha means enlightened. Enlightenment is unobscured, immaterial light appearance with the quality of limitless, positive wisdom energy. That is the meaning of Buddhas, deities, and sublime beings.

In both the Mahāyāna and Vajrayāna traditions, enlightenment is the state of the three kāyas. Even if Buddhas and deities are named differently according to the way that their innumerable qualities are discerned, their essence is always the wisdom of enlightenment, which is Dharmakāya, always indivisible from its unobstructed manifestation as the immeasurable qualities of Sambhogakāya and Nirmānakāya. Since Dharmakāya is stainless, their manifestation in form must be stainless, no matter which aspect occurs. This is called Buddha according to the Mahāyāna tradition, and called deity according to the Vajrayāna tradition.

If a particular Buddha or deity is selected with dualistic favoritism and others are excluded, it impedes and limits the recognition of the immeasurable qualities of Nirmānakāya and Sambhogakāya. This is not seeing and knowing Buddhas and deities, but just substantializing them by the projections and contrivances of sentient beings' conceptions of worldly, supernatural form. Because it makes a division, it does not lead to enlightenment, since anything that is divided is substance and always falls apart and diminishes.

All Buddhas and deities are contained within each Buddha and deity. Also, from each Buddha and deity, all immeasurable Buddhas and deities are manifesting. In the sky of Dharmadhātu, awareness wisdom is always effortlessly manifesting.

All Buddhas are the three kāyas. Buddha Śakyamuni is always in stainless Dharmakāya, so therefore he is always abiding in immeasurable Sambhogakāya purelands and always emanating in many different Nirmānakāya aspects.

Dharmakāya is indestructible and indivisible, so when one visualizes Buddha Śakyamuni in the form of a pure monk, other Buddhas cannot be excluded. All Buddhas, including all wisdom ḍākinīs, are contained within his body, speech, and mind. According to general phenomena, Buddha Śakyamuni is robed as a monk, signifying that he has abandoned all worldly, desirable qualities which are the source and objects of attachment according to the Hīnayāna point of view. Yet, since he is Buddha, all immeasurable Buddhas must be contained within him. This includes even those Buddhas whose qualities seem incompatible with his aspect as a monk, such as wisdom ḍākinīs, which sounds strange to those who are attached to a strict form of merely material morality. Ḍākinī means immaculate śūnyatā, which is Dharmakāya. Since Dharmakāya is immaculate, it manifests freely, so it is flawless exaltation, so it is wisdom ḍākinī. Wisdom is the origin of inexhaustible qualities and is not limited to some certain form. When we offer all desirable qualities to all Buddhas and ḍākinīs, we receive their wisdom blessings through our faith. If we truly want to open our minds to attain enlightenment, there is no conflict between the myriad forms of the Buddhas, whether they manifest as free from desire, such as Buddha Śakyamuni, or as full of flawless, desirable qualities, such as Sambhogakāya deities.

According to the Hīnayāna point of view, Buddha Śakyamuni has abandoned ego and the passions and attained the enlightenment of self-peace. According to the Mahāyāna point of view, Buddha has purified all obscurations of the passions and cognition and attained the full enlightenment of supreme omniscience. According to the Vajrayāna point of view, Buddha is indestructibly, beginninglessly enlightened. All of the different aspects in which he is enlightened, whether wearing the robes of a monk or ornamented with jewels, with an expression of wrath or an expression of tranquillity, and whether male or female, are the reflections of the capacities of sentient beings. These reflections are not limitations of Buddha, who has no possessive mind that attaches itself to particular qualities. They are simply the qualities of Buddha's unobstructed wisdom body. Since Buddha is enlightened from whatever view is taken, he can manifest anything without intention.

In the same way, when we visualize Padmasambhava in the aspect of a vajramaster, we must think that all immeasurable Buddhas, including Buddha Śakyamuni, are contained within his body, speech, and mind, because Padmasambhava is Dharmakāya, Sambhogakāya, and Nirmānakāya. There is no separation between all Buddhas. If we have this point of view, we will not cause contradictions between manifestations of Buddhas, and we will be inspired to unite with all Buddhas.

According to the Mahāyāna teachings, Buddha nature exists until attaining full enlightenment. Those whose Buddha nature is blossoming through practice in order to attain enlightenment for the benefit of all beings are called Bodhisattvas. When full enlightenment is attained, there is not even the name of Buddha nature, because there is nothing left of ordinary mind that can be differentiated from Buddha nature. There is only Buddha. Buddhas effortlessly benefit sentient beings through the result of their previous great effort and vast intention as Bodhisattvas.

According to the Vajrayāna teachings, Buddha nature is called inherently born wisdom deity. This is because even though beings are momentarily obscured by ordinary mind and do not recognize it, deity is within mind and nowhere else. In order for inherently born wisdom deity to blossom, practice with wisdom and its pure phenomena is continuous until attaining the full enlightenment of wisdom deity maṇḍala. Those whose inherently born wisdom deity is blossoming through practice to attain full enlightenment for the benefit of all sentient beings are called yogis and yoginis. When full enlightenment is attained, there is not even the name of inherently born deity, because there is nothing left of ordinary mind that can be differentiated from inherently born deity. There is only self-adorned, immeasurable wisdom deity maṇḍala.

If we do not let inherently born wisdom deity, which is pure mind, blossom through the guidance of wisdom teachers so it remains dormant for many lives, dualistic propensities will be strengthened. That strengthened energy causes many ordinary, substantial phenomena which sometimes seem to result in unhappiness and sometimes in happiness. This creates continuous hope for more substantial happiness and dread of unhappiness, causing continuous rejection and acceptance between object and subject. One harms oneself and other beings through the egoism of trying to sabotage and defeat others in order to create more self-substantializing power and to concretize one's ego. This obscuration continuously causes disturbances. It is the ignorance which prevents peace and the attaining of enlightenment. It does not matter if one is born sometimes in lower realms and sometimes in higher realms; either way, liberation from suffering is prevented by the preoccupations of ordinary ego. Unless the power of inherently born deity is strengthened through recognition and practice to attain enlightenment, there is always evil caused by the energy of dualistic ego. Through forgetting that all projections, reactions, and reprojections have the root of ego, evil seems to come from outside of oneself as many different kinds of forms and sounds. Actually, evil only seems to have an independent, external existence because one forgets what one's demonic ego has created by building evil habits over many lives, not recognizing one's projections. If mind is unaware, it does not know anything about what it is causing either momentarily or ultimately.

If we can, we should practice and realize inherently born wisdom deity according to the teachings of our tradition until reaching self-correcting confidence, which means not being influenced by previous ordinary, negative habit or by unenlightened, inverted spiritual beings in the present or any future lives, until attaining enlightenment. Full enlightenment is the total annihilation of all countless samsaric projections of negative energy, because there is no power of duality.

Whenever wisdom mind is not recognized, there are countless projections of countless sentient beings with dualistic mind and its habits. At the same time, within countless sentient beings' minds, there are countless inherently born wisdom deities. If one's own mind remains in ordinary duality, there are always the countless, ordinary phenomena of sentient beings. But if one's own inherently born wisdom deities blossom through recognition and practice, one's own phenomena of other sentient beings will not exist, because they are transformed through self-apotheosis to the inherent wisdom of each sentient being. When one's own wisdom blossoms, other sentient beings' inherently born wisdom deities blossom, since other sentient beings are one's own phenomena. So all is fully enlightened at once into oneness, without even a single, ordinary sentient being remaining. From oneness, infinite, immeasurable, pure, insubstantial wisdom maṇḍala manifests.

Some people misunderstand the wrathful activities of subduing, annihilating, and conquering mudras in the histories and sādhanas of Buddhist tantric deities, thinking that they are harmful. However, according to the phenomena of Buddhas, wrathfulness is only wisdom activity. Because Buddhas do not have dualistic phenomena, there is no object that can be harmed or subject that is wrathful.

If an audience watches a magician killing beings on a stage in a theater, the audience knows his magic is only a performance and not real. But sometimes, even though the people in the audience know the magician is not killing anyone, they may have fear through their own habit of reality and react as though he really were. Actually, the magician does not have any conception of killing, or even any phenomena of magic.

Wisdom magic has no grasping mind. It is only a manifestation to other beings who believe in the phenomena of reality, showing what appear to be reality's activities in order to guide them beyond reality and unreality. When sublime beings appear to be wrathful, it is just the natural, limitless display of wisdom mind, occurring as sentient beings' reflections appearing in front of them. Then, through wrathful or peaceful appearances of enlightened display, sentient beings can connect to wisdom and one day attain enlightenment.

In order not to have any dualistic phenomena, we have to subdue our own habit of duality. The subduer is wisdom, and the object of subjugation is dualistic appearance. According to Buddhas' phenomena, there is no object to be subdued because wisdom has no dual habit. But according to our own phenomena, we must annihilate dualistic habit through wisdom by practicing. The meaning of this is to try to destroy all conception in order to be liberated from saṃsāra. Dualistic appearances become like a demon we annihilate with the point of view of wisdom deity.

Ordinary harm belongs to the reality phenomena of sentient beings. In the stainless wrath of dharmatā, there is not even an iota of a chance for the interference of the source of all harm, dualistic conception. There is only the natural wrathfulness of Dharmakāya, which is most peaceful. From that natural, nondualistic quality, unobstructed manifestations can occur as immeasurable Sambhogakāya wrathful and peaceful deities, which, instead of causing suffering, are full of immeasurable exaltation Buddhafields. From that state, manifesting peacefulness in order to harmonize with peaceful sentient beings, manifesting desirable qualities in order to satisfy lustful sentient beings, or manifesting wrath in order to subdue cruel beings, these deities only benefit to guide beyond peace, lust, or wrath. This is the origin of inconceivably wrathful, peaceful enlightenment.

Therefore, the meaning of the wrathful activities of deities is to subdue beings by their own reflection, introducing their own negative conceptions in order to conquer them through their own positive wrathful aspect. The meaning is not to kill other reality beings within the reality of subject and object. In the same way, peacefulness and joining in union with desirable consorts are also one's own manifestation, and must occur with sentient beings' own reflection.

Through lack of recognition and faith in the wisdom wrath and peace of their own actual enlightened mind, and through grasping, sentient beings create aspects of wrath and peace within reality, which are always causing the suffering of reality. By not abiding in the state of the natural wrathfulness of Dharmakāya, which is most peaceful, the manifestation of peaceful qualities becomes the attachment of subject and object, and the manifestation of wrathful qualities becomes the aversion of subject and object, so there is always attachment and aversion in saṃsāra. As everyone knows, sentient beings are always unavoidably harming each other, whether directly or indirectly. It is not always necessary to connect harming with material weapons. If someone feels and says he has been hurt, it means that he feels someone has damaged him. From small injuries up to murder and war, without any antidote from a wisdom point of view, harm is continuous.

In many histories of sublime beings and also in many sādhanas, the annihilation of evil beings is mentioned. The meaning of this activity is completely different from ordinary harm; it is to end the continuous creation of negative karma by evil beings, which will lead to their suffering in lower realms, and instead to guide them toward enlightenment with limitless compassion. It is foolish to make the misinterpretation that wrathful wisdom activities are a negative creation of religion. Obviously, as long as there are the phenomena of subject and object in the universe, there is always harm at different times and places. The only variation is in whether it momentarily appears or does not appear according to karmic result. Even if beings do not believe in harming in order to annihilate dualistic habit, negative activities unavoidably exist within beings' phenomena. For example, all countries of the human realm, whether they are small or big, cultured or uncultured, always have protectors who guard against harm. This has always been so, which shows that harm has always happened and is not an invention or tradition of Buddhism.

All religions have some form of meditation, even though their points of view are different, which means they want suffering to cease and that they recognize suffering is caused by conception. By not allowing conceptions to arise through meditation, all conceptions cease in equanimity. Actually, this is trying to kill conception, even though it may seem strange to hear this unusual way of describing it. In brief, practice means to annihilate the suffering samsaric beings created by dualistic conception. If one does not want to kill conception, then one cannot even meditate, since meditation is the cessation

of the conception of grasping mind, which is the actual object of killing. Without doing this, one actually causes continuous reality killing
because one causes continuous dualistic habit.

When wrathful or semiwrathful deities are shown in statues
and paintings drinking blood from a skullcup, the meaning is not to
harm reality's sentient beings by using their blood for worship. The
meaning of a skullcup of blood is the suffering of saṃsāra. Wisdom
deities drink this blood of samsaric suffering as a gesture of liberating
samsaric beings from samsaric habit to the inseparability of nondualistic exaltation. We must pray to be fortunate enough to hear this kind
of vast teaching, rather than having a wrong point of view or para-
noia. Without this great point of view it is impossible to liberate the
samsaric skandhas. Practice means to murder all of saṃsāra. It does
not matter if this is done with tranquil eyes in the samādhi of peaceful
deities, or with staring eyes in the samādhi of wrathful deities. The
main point of view is to annihilate immeasurable saṃsāra.

Sometimes corpses are shown under the feet of wrathful deities
who are stepping on them. Depending on the sādhana, these corpses
sometimes represent one's own ordinary five skandhas being destroyed; one's consciousness is transformed into deity, and one's ordinary habit of form becomes like a powerless corpse. Sometimes
corpses are symbolic of supernatural worldly gods who are very powerful, but not beneficial for liberating sentient beings to enlightenment. Even though these worldly gods have the power to give some
common siddhi, they can only create worldly power which causes
suffering since they have no egoless wisdom mind. Their corpses
show that they are subdued by wisdom herukas.

Also, sometimes statues or paintings are made according to histories or sādhanas in which Buddhist tantric deities are holding the
heads of eternalist gods in their hands. This does not mean that particular eternalist gods are being killed with hatred, although some
people have taken these images literally and think that Buddhist deities are being shown murdering their gods. The meaning is that there
are no more gods of eternalism, which are connected with ego. If

there is ego, including supernatural ego, other beings can be harmed. If there is no ultimate wisdom, these supernatural gods can cause conflicts of power, creating supernatural ego instead of wisdom, and causing suffering instead of liberation. Enlightenment has no ego. Ego can harm sentient beings, so it must be annihilated. That is why when we practice, we have to follow the meaning of this speech of Rigdzin Jigmed Lingpa:

> I, a yogi performing fearless activity
> By sustaining the understanding of the pervasive equanimity
> of saṃsāra and nirvāṇa,
> Dance on the supernatural gods and evil of grasping mind
> And annihilate the devil of dualistic grasping into ashes.

Many people misunderstand the aspect of the union of deities because of their wrong point of view, their habit of grabbing at morality, and their creation of concrete, inert moral ego, which causes immorality. That is why Buddha has named self-righteous moral ego. If one grasps excessively at morality, it causes immorality, because attachment to one's own purity builds ego, and whatever builds ego causes saṃsāra again. According to tantric tradition, the union of deities and offerings of desirable qualities are appearances within form that show how to accept and acknowledge immeasurable, sublime exaltation. The main meaning of union is indivisible emptiness and exaltation, and the sign of this is the mudrā of female and male deity united. Even within one's own mind, there is emptiness and exaltation because mind does not have any reality or source of suffering, since a source of suffering cannot be found, which is the origin of exaltation. So exaltation manifests sometimes as the form of female deity, sometimes as the form of male deity, and sometimes as the forms of male and female deities in union, according to the faculties and karmic connections of beings.

It is unnecessary to think of union as only between men and women, or that union is negative. Whenever there are two things, it means that they can join together. It is unnecessary to particularly disapprove of males and females joining together. Ordinary union always exists within saṃsāra. Also, all religions automatically contain union. Religions have to have some form of practice since otherwise they would have no purpose, and any religious practice is joining two things, creating union. Union means joining together to create exaltation. When people pray, it is in order to join with their god to receive blessing. Blessing is giving exaltation, and if exaltation is received, it means union. If one disapproves of religious union between deities as immoral, one must instead first disapprove of the union between all males and females in the universe, because the union of deities is the phenomena of sentient beings. The origin of union is not immorality from deities but is the phenomena of beings, so if one wanted to stop union, one would first have to stop the phenomena of beings through meditation, or union, which is the only way.

Some people think that although one being has emptied his own samsaric phenomena by becoming enlightened, other beings' samsaric phenomena still exist. But if people think that way, it is just a sign of not believing in their own inherently born wisdom deity and choosing to save and adore their dualistic habit in a precious way. For those who are enlightened, there is not even an iota of a conception of beings, of practice, or of an essence. But even though there is no object of dedication, the power of the unobstructed compassion of enlightenment is naturally pervasive because it is the natural quality of wisdom.

The idea of an essence or of anything that is intrinsic, innate, inherent, or potential is only used according to the basis and the path. As Buddha Śakyamuni said in *The Glorious Rosary Sound of the Lion Sūtra*:

> When the bud of the complete wisdom body of Buddha has not opened because of temporary stains, it is called Buddha nature.

Also, as Nāgārjuna said:

> When it is springtime,
> People say water is warm.

In wintertime,
They say it is cold.
Likewise, when Buddha nature is covered by the nest of
    the passions,
It is called sentient beings.
When Buddha nature is separated from the passions,
It is called Buddha.

When elightenment is attained, an essence or any other inner-most quality cannot be said to exist, because this would indicate that there was something which could be distinguished, extracted, or dis-tilled from something else, which implies duality. According to the basis and the path, there is dualistic mind and there is nondualistic mind, so we encourage nondualistic mind to open, which is the es-sence of Buddhas and deities. But according to the result, there is no essence that is inside, which would mean that there is something else that is outside. Since Buddhas and deities do not have any duality or anything that can be separated from something else, there is not something to choose and something else to try to remove. Buddhas and deities are the sole unity of enlightenment, so there is nothing that can be made into an essence that can be differentiated. There is not even anything that can be transformed from one state to another, since whichever aspect of deity manifests is always the three kāyas and does not need to become anything else.

When there is no obscuration and all appearances are wisdom, it is actual deity. Whether one wants to make one's own phenomena into dualistic habit or the enlightened appearance of wisdom deities is not decided outwardly; it is one's own choice.

Wisdom deities are not coming from outside of oneself like outer objects or from an inner subject ego; they come from one's own wis-dom. In whatever forms they appear, they are self-reflections. From this point of view, ordinary dualistic mind is not even accepted. There is just the temporary obscuration of habit through not recognizing wisdom mind, so it is only called ordinary mind, but it does not really exist. In order to attain enlightenment, which is the state of wisdom maṇḍala, one's own mind must be recognized as stainless, immeasurable space, not made by anyone, not coming from anywhere, not only manifesting from time to time, but always unconditional wisdom without intention. By practicing one's sādhana with this point of view, there is no thought of one's ordinary house, ordinary body, or ordinary beings, because all houses are wisdom palaces, all outer elements are immeasurable exaltation elements, and all forms are immeasurable wisdom forms. This is the natural wisdom ecstasy of deity, which is the state of Vajradhāra in which all immeasurable Buddhas are contained within immeasurable wisdom maṇḍala.

Wisdom deity is pure space. Space is deathless because there is no object to seize. Space is tranquil because it is unconditioned. Space is pervasive because its unobstructed activity is everywhere. Wisdom deity is wherever there is awareness light pureland and its effortless manifestations with the immortal ecstasy of wisdom.

In kriyā tantra, it is called the deity of Dharmatā because it is naturally pure. In upa tantra, it is called the deity of absolute space because it is completely limitless. In yoga tantra, it is called the deity of the completely stainless aspect of space because it is awareness mind's quality of immeasurable, immaculate wisdom. In mahāyoga, it is called the immeasurable pervasiveness of purity because it is the boundless radiance of the expanse of awareness wisdom.

Self-manifesting supreme wisdom deity is uncompounded like sky. It is natural, uncontrived, pure wisdom from the beginning and the self-accomplishment of supreme siddhi. Wisdom does not come from any conditions and is always clear light because it is unobstructed. Whatever comes from wisdom is self-wish-fulfilling.

Even though different terms are used according to the incalculable aspects of qualities of deities, the pith of the point of view of deities is nondualistic wisdom awareness mind, because it does not cause any diminishable, substantial phenomena but only ineffable, infallible wisdom energy with indestructible, celestial purelands. Its nature is substanceless like inexpressible, stainless sky, so there is not even the name of death because it is never born. Also, it is not like just empty sky, because it is always the immeasurable, unobstructed, pure wisdom appearances of light body, speech, mind, quality, and activity, and inconceivable, empyreal Buddhafields with the flawless qualities of exaltation.

When, for one indefinite moment, we borrow this guesthouse human body, we must take advantage of our good fortune and follow sublime beings. In order to not sink in the quicksand of saṃsāra and to awaken wisdom, we must study and listen to the teachings and histories of sublime beings. Since all deviations from original purity are included within the two extremes of nihilism and eternalism, unless we can recognize the state of Samantabhadra, we go back and forth continuously between sometimes being born with nihilist habits and sometimes being born with eternalist habits. For this reason, nihilist and eternalist habits must be identified as what they are and purified. In order to benefit all beings, these dualistic habits must be transformed into Samantabhadra's mind, the same as Kunkhyen Longchenpa's mind, which is nondualistic, free wisdom space, so that we may attain the meaning of these words:

> Oneself and others are Samantabhadra,
> Eternalism and nihilism are Samantabhadra.
> In the expanse of Samantabhadra,
> There is no self, other, eternalism, or nihilism.
>
> — KUNKHYEN LONGCHENPA

The Senses

This Meeting, as in a Dream

As in a dream, when cuckoos start to sing, it is spring. When I awoke on the first spring day, I remembered my dream that when the sense object meets the sense, that is the echo.

It is so magical, it is so wondrous that I dreamed the dream that echoed the substanceless essence of the substanceless dream.

Untouchable dream. Uncatchable echo.

O Lord Buddha, through your blessing did you dream for me to show that all phenomena are illusory like a dream and cannot be caught?

In summertime, when peacocks' tails make parasols, I met a celestial ḍākinī without invitation in my dream.

It is so magical, it is so wondrous, this meeting, as in a dream.

In autumntime, when the meadow dew, like tears, meets the moonbeams' wistful love, I watched the falling leaves and remembered my dream that when the sense object meets the sense, that is the echo.

It is so magical, it is so wondrous, this meeting, as in a dream.

In wintertime, when the wind thief's whispered lament meets the snow-faced earth holder of wealth, my mind grew weary.

It is so magical, it is so wondrous, this meeting, as in a dream.

All sentient beings, including myself, take all that is perceived to be real and do not recognize that when the sense object meets the sense, that is the echo.

Whatever is seen as the object of the eyes that is unpleasant causes repulsion, and whatever is seen as the object of the eyes that is pleasant causes desire. Between repulsion and desire, rejection and acceptance are caused, which is the source of suffering.

Whatever is heard as the object of the ears that is unpleasant causes repulsion, and whatever is heard as the object of the ears that is pleasant causes desire. Between repulsion and desire, rejection and acceptance are caused, which is the source of suffering.

Whatever is smelled as the object of the nose that is unpleasant causes repulsion, and whatever is smelled as the object of the nose that is pleasant causes desire. Between repulsion and desire, rejection and acceptance are caused, which is the source of suffering.

Whatever is tasted as the object of the tongue that is unpleasant causes repulsion, and whatever is tasted as the object of the tongue that is pleasant causes desire. Between repulsion and desire, rejection and acceptance are caused, which is the source of suffering.

Whatever is felt as the object of touch that is unpleasant causes repulsion, and whatever is felt as the object of touch that is pleasant causes desire. Between repulsion and desire, rejection and acceptance are caused, which is the source of suffering.

We forget my dream that when the sense object meets the sense, that is the echo.

Through their technology, scientists strive to find the source of the sense object's substance, splitting it smaller and smaller until smallest of small cannot be further split. They look for the source of the object, ignoring the source of the subject.

Between subject and object, they are suffering, because they forget my dream that when the sense object meets the sense, that is the echo.

Through their introspection, philosophers strive to find the source of the substanceless subject. Ignoring their unconditioned wisdom mind, they read and write, deduce and conclude, making new conditions and conceptions, new subtle substance which, lighter and lighter, rises like mist in the clear open sky, collecting in dense substance clouds which spill heavy rain back down to earth.

Between light sky and heavy earth, they are suffering, because they forget my dream that when the sense object meets the sense, that is the echo.

Through their medicine, doctors strive to cure sickness, never understanding the connection between inner and outer elements which creates disease. Fixing one part, they ignore the whole, like a bad carpenter who repairs the ceiling while the floor is caving in, or like a tree surgeon who cuts the branches of a poisoned tree while the poison remains in the root.

Between impairing and repairing, they are suffering, because they forget my dream that when the sense object meets the sense, that is the echo.

Through their ordinary mind's understanding, psychologists strive to cure patients of ordinary mind's problems. Curious to cure their object of concern, they practice without wisdom channels, never knowing their wisdom mind. Like babysitters with children, they offer toys to temporarily stop their momentary crying. Their expectation-to-cure mind is uncertain and their limited, intellectual method cannot adapt to the patients' changing circumstances. Like a bad fortuneteller, they fear that their divinations will not work.

Between fearing and hoping, they are suffering, because they forget my dream that when the sense object meets the sense, that is the echo.

Through their concentration, meditators strive to destroy bad conception saṃsāra and good conception nirvāṇa. Sitting in samādhi, they escape from their external, turbulent city, but still, their fearless lion awareness is lost. Even though their posture is restful, their watcher cat is tired from not catching their countless lives' hurry-habit-rat conceptions.

Between depending on watcher cat and catchless rat thoughts, they are suffering, because they forget my dream that when the sense object meets the sense, that is the echo.

It is so magical, it is so wondrous, this meeting, as in a dream.

The immaculate wisdom senses of the Buddhas manifest from completely pure elements. There is no curtain of cognitive obscurations. Each wisdom sense contains the limitless qualities of every other wisdom sense, and can discern each and every aspect of all appearance simultaneously and without distortion. Sentient beings have the same pure senses as the Buddhas, but they grasp at their self-reflection, trying to possess it instead of abiding in the noncontradiction of wisdom. Through not recognizing the quality of unobstructedness, these reflections become divided into the subject that possesses and the object that is possessed. Because of this division, phenomena are misinterpreted and the pure light elements become obscured and tangible. From these tangible elements, the sediment of the residual karmic energy of dualistic mind compounds into each of the ordinary senses.

For human beings, the sense gatherings are caused by the unawakened basis of ordinary dualistic mind and phenomena. According to the Hīnayāna teachings, there are six sense gatherings of seeing, hearing, smelling, tasting, touching, and consciousness. According to the Mahāyāna teachings of Yogācāra, there are eight sense gatherings which also include the consciousness of the passions and the basis of consciousness. The senses may arise differently in other realms, according to the karmic energy of beings.

Each sense gathering is the conjoining of the sense organ, the consciousness of the sense, and the object of the sense. Depending on intention, these senses can become limited and obscured when they are misused to create saṃsāra, or they can be transformed into clear, unimpeded senses to reach enlightenment.

The source of the senses is mind, and the nature of mind is always unobstructed. The ordinary senses are only an expression of fragmented consciousness within different forms, times, and places. When the limitation of these forms, times, and places is purified through believing in Buddha nature and meditation, wisdom senses are attained. This state has no different form, time, or place, manifesting unobstructed power according to different beings' faculties of form, time, and place.

All of the senses are formed from the potentials of the five elements. If there is no potential quality of earth, the elements cannot obtain form. If there is no potential quality of water, the elements cannot collect. If there is no potential quality of fire, the elements cannot ripen. If there is no potential quality of air, the elements cannot increase. If there is no potential quality of space, the elements cannot develop.

When an embryo is formed, it relies on all five elements. At that time, the mother should not run, jump, or do any hard work. The three causes of pregnancy are the father's pure sperm, the mother's pure ovum, and karma. The potential of the inner elements exists in these three causes.

The father's sperm predominantly causes bones, and the mother's ovum predominantly causes flesh and blood. When the potential of the earth element is achieved, the hard substances such as the flesh and bones of the body are formed, and the sense of smell and sense object of smell develop.

When the potential of the water element is achieved, the liquids of the body such as the blood are formed, and the sense of taste and sense object of taste develop.

When the potential of the fire element is achieved, the warmth of the body is formed, giving the body its complexion, and the sense of sight and sense object of sight develop. Even though the organ of the eye is connected with the water element, the essence of light and sight are connected with the fire element because light causes clarity and appearance. This fire is not an ordinary, burning fire, but luminous, clear light.

When the potential of the air element is achieved, the breath of the body is formed, and the sense of touch and sense object of touch develop.

When the potential of the space element is achieved, energy flows, which is opened by space, and the sense of hearing and sense object of hearing develop.

Although most beings have some senses which are clearer than others, it is very difficult for one being to perfect all of the senses within one body because of the obscurations of habit. The differences in sentient beings' senses are not the result of coincidence, but of differences in the ways that karmic sediment was previously caused and imbalances in the elements were created. Positive habits cause positive karma that results in a clearer and more unobscured mind and a karmic body with clearer and more unobscured senses. When beings have created positive, spiritual energy through their senses in previous lives, they perceive the objects of the senses more clearly.

Different beings can have very different experiences of the same phenomena because of the differences in their senses. For example, even when students have the same teachers, study the same subjects, and receive the same instructions at the same time, some learn more quickly than others because their previous habits have resulted in clear senses. Since mind is the unobstructed source of the senses, it is the creator of all phenomena. If mind is left in fragmented, nihilist habit, the senses through which the mind functions are clouded and phenomena become contorted. When their senses are clear, the discernment of philosophers is more incisive, the comprehension of scientists is more acute, the creativity of artists is more refined, the therapy of psychologists is more helpful, the faith of religious people is deeper, and the spiritual phenomena of Buddhists are sublime.

We can only perceive one thing at a time when we use mind's habit of delusion with the ordinary senses. We may think we can perceive different objects at the same time with our ordinary mind, but we are actually perceiving them separately in a sequence of instants. When we focus clearly with a particular sense, the clarity of our other senses becomes dormant; and when we focus clearly on a particular object, the clarity of our perception of other objects becomes dormant.

Within one ordinary mind, there are countless conceptions which create countless divisions. However many divisions there are, there are that many obstructions of the senses. However many obstructions there are, that much cannot be perceived of different places and different times. However much our view of place and time is blocked, that much cannot be known of limitless direction, place, and time.

We have countless samsaric perceptions and ordinary phenomena because we misuse our senses with the divisions of our countless conceptions. Nevertheless, these conceptions are also an indication of our potentially limitless, unobscured senses and pure phenomena. Since we perceive according to our conceptions, if our conceptions are limited, then our perceptions will be limited. Instead, we can create the basis of limitlessness, transforming all of our phenomena into unobstructed, radiant wisdom appearance.

Even though different names are used for the functioning of the senses through the mind, all senses originate in mind, and there is only one mind. When mind becomes light, it is more vast and clear because it can perceive many different objects directly and simultaneously. If we practice with light energy which comes from light mind, it is possible to begin to perceive the objects of all of the senses without contradiction, so that past, present, and future place and time can be known. When the divisions between subject and object and between one sense and another vanish, the light of enlightened mind shines everywhere limitlessly, the same as Buddha's, whose omniscient vision is always flawless.

Nihilists do not accept the continuous basis of mind as the origin of all the phenomena of relative truth, including the senses. They only acknowledge the effect of the meeting of the senses themselves with the objects of the senses. Even though nihilists do not deny that the senses function through mind, they believe that the senses, their perceptions, any objective phenomena perceived, and mind itself only exist within a basis of physical form as a result of coincidental circumstances. They do not believe that mind continues to exist beyond death in other lives, in tangible physical bodies, or in intangible mental bodies. They just believe in what is apparent to them within the tangible creations of dualistic grasping that separates phenomena from mind, so they always find objects that are divided from subjects.

Nihilists generally believe that mind originates from substantial elements when circumstances come together to produce living beings. They believe that consciousness is dependent on the life which comes from these inert elements. Buddhists believe that mind is independent of the elements, and that substance has no potential to produce mind even though mind can connect to the elements and appear within substance. The Buddhist point of view is that the ordinary elements of the phenomena of substance are created from the habit of mind, and are only its reflections. Unlike nihilists who think that the forms of living beings are determined by their genetic heritage, Buddhists believe that mind creates habit, and habit creates living beings and realms of existence that can arise in any form depending on the aspect of the habit that mind creates, unless continuous mind is transformed into unending wisdom mind, free from dualistic conceptions.

According to many different nihilist, religious, philosophical, medical, psychological, artistic, and even some eternalist tantric ideas, mind is found within the body. However, as long as beings are trapped by dualistic mind, wherever mind seems to be found is only an expression of the experience of the senses. The karmic habit of the senses determines what is perceived; and whatever is perceived through the senses will seem true, even though ordinary senses only perceive relative, temporary phenomena. But mind, the source of the senses, cannot be found within any of the senses of the body or anywhere within substance.

If mind existed somewhere, then it would have to exist within the five skandhas of form, feeling, perception, intention, and consciousness. Yet no matter how much we examine the five skandhas in order to find the mind, we cannot find it in any of them.

Although the senses arise from the mind, mind itself cannot be confined to any of the senses. It is like light carried by karmic air in the channels of the body through which the senses function. Yet even though the channels of the body carry the energy of the mind, we cannot find the mind within any of them. Since mind is inconceivable light, it cannot be found anywhere, but it becomes consciousness when it is contained in the channels of the senses and their objects, just like the imperceptible potential of light becomes perceptible when it is channeled through a lamp. Because mind is the origin of the channels, airs, and essence, it is connected to them as long as it remains in saṃsāra. That is why many precious Buddhist tantric teachings show how to purify ordinary mind through the channels, airs, and essence by the recognition of wisdom deity so that the ordinary elements of the karmic senses are transformed into the immaculate elements of the wisdom senses.

We must not think that the connection which exists between the senses and the object of the senses is always apparent. Their connection may be dormant until circumstances arise to bring them together. This connection arises through karmic air whenever the senses and the object of the senses come together, just as fire dormant in embers under ashes springs into flames when it is fed with wood and blown by the wind.

When we perceive objects through our sense of sight, we do not notice the air between our eyes and the objects of sight because we have the habit of not perceiving form when it is not visible. We do not recognize that what is there is invisible form.

When we perceive objects through our sense of hearing, we do not notice the air between our ears and the objects of hearing because we have the habit of not perceiving air when it is not audible. We do not recognize that what is there is inaudible sound.

When we perceive objects through our sense of smell, we do not notice the air between our nose and the objects of smell because we have the habit of not perceiving air when it does not have an odor. We do not recognize that what is there is odorless smell.

When we perceive objects through our sense of taste, we do not recognize the air between our tongue and the objects of taste because we have the habit of not perceiving air when it has no flavor. We do not recognize that what is there is flavorless taste.

When we perceive objects through our sense of touch, we do not notice the air between our fingers and the objects of touch because we have the habit of not perceiving air when it is not touchable. We do not recognize that what is there is untouchable form.

Mind's intention is the origin of the basic, natural movement which is called air, but this does not mean that mind only causes the outer air of wind or the inner air of breath. Any outer or inner waves of the immeasurable phenomena of all existence are caused by the natural movement of mind and cannot appear without it. This natural movement exists wherever the mind focuses.

Unless we practice and awareness mind becomes completely unconditioned as it originally is, ordinary mind depends on the ordinary elements and follows the movement of obscured karmic air uncontrollably. If we do not practice, ordinary mind is like someone who is disabled and cannot travel by himself, karmic air is like a blind horse he depends on which takes him everywhere without any certain destination, and the channels of the senses are like the road they take. If we are not mindful, the karmic air of previous habit has the power to carry the mind everywhere. Even at a worldly level, the communication between subject and object, and between personal and general phenomena, misses the target and can cause disaster. When we are mindful, we can control the karmic air and direct it to our chosen positive destination by focusing and using the channels of our senses at the right time and on the right path.

Because karmic air always goes to a certain place, the senses must follow its course, like an irrigation conduit that only flows in one direction. But if we practice, the channels of the senses are directed by mindfulness, and we can transcend the limitation of the direction of their karmic path. Buddha's wisdom senses do not have ordinary, constricted karmic passageways. In order to ascend to the state of Buddha, practitioners try to purify karmic air and to recognize wisdom air which naturally arises with practice, so that the obscured perceptions of the ordinary senses can be transformed into the all-knowing awareness of the wisdom senses.

Ordinary karmic channels are like a net that encompasses and restrains the karmic body. If karmic channels are purified through practice, then wisdom manifestations are unobstructed. This is Nirmānakāya.

Ordinary karmic air is like pollution that depletes pure energy and causes heaviness. If karmic air is purified through practice, then immeasurable stainless wisdom sound and clear light Buddhafields pervade. This is Sambhogakāya.

Ordinary mind is like an insect trapped in its own spittle. If ordinary mind is purified through practice, then sole great tigle is totally unobscured. This is Dharmakāya.

In order to be liberated from suffering and to not allow the influence of the outer objects of the senses, or to be manipulated by one's own senses, one is supposed to introspect and watch the way that rejection and acceptance occur within the senses, circumstances, and time, looking inwardly toward one's own consciousness of the senses until the senses and the consciousness of the senses become untarnished. The benefit of doing this is that one does not become emotional and disturbed by repulsive and desirable phenomena and by the effort of rejection and acceptance within circumstance and time, and that one's mind becomes stable and tranquil. Ultimately, one can attain the stainless wisdom senses of Dharmakāya mind. That is why one saint said:

> When I am among many people, I watch what is arising
>   from my senses.
> When I am alone, I leave my mind in naked awareness.

The meaning of Dharma, if it is put into one simple word, is holding phenomena. This means all phenomena, including anything tangible or intangible that can be known and named. The way in which phenomena are held is up to each being. The impure phenomena of saṃsāra are held by grasping mind, and the pure phenomena of inconceivable Buddha qualities are held by nondualistic wisdom mind, which is holding the lineage of wisdom. If phenomena are constricted through the limited perception of the ordinary senses, the passions arise and cause karma. When phenomena are recognized as the inconceivable affluence of wisdom senses, Buddhahood is attained.

All the phenomena of our senses are only the result of our habit. We can understand the nature of the different kinds of habit and how they are created by recognizing this. Whenever spiritual habit is dormant, nihilist habit arises so that the senses only perceive what is tangible. Yet even when there is no conception of spiritual qualities, they exist potentially within the basis of mind.

Whenever nihilist habit is dormant, tangible and intangible spiritual habit can arise and the senses which are influenced by this habit can perceive both substantial and insubstantial spiritual phenomena. Even though there are many realms which have supernatural beings with supernatural senses who do not have nihilist habit, these beings are still not enlightened. In whatever realms beings exist, when their spiritual qualities arise, they can use tangible and intangible energy among other beings in either a demonic way with harmful senses or in a godly way with beneficial senses. Of course, demonic senses cannot benefit. Even godly senses cannot benefit ultimately if they are based on the ego's spiritual energy.

Even if phenomena seem to be spiritual, when they do not cause enlightenment, they are only aspects of the countless forms of deluded samsaric habit. Any phenomena that occur with the power of grasping, dualistic ego do not release us from saṃsāra. Whether phenomena seem to be nihilist or spiritual, they are still worldly when created by ordinary, shortsighted senses, because ordinary senses relating to ordinary objects only cause ordinary phenomena.

The purpose of increasing the pure spiritual energy of the senses is to break the ordinary habit which continuously keeps beings in saṃsāra. The influence of Buddha's precious teachings diminishes nihilist habit and ordinary spiritual habit so that the previous positive karmic connection to our Buddha nature mind can blossom and pure spiritual energy can manifest. This spiritual energy is not influenced either by nihilist habit or by the ordinary spiritual habit of ego. It leads beyond habit to enlightenment through the purification of obscurations, the accumulation of virtue, and the recognition of Buddha nature.

If we practice, many wisdom appearances will arise as a sign that the senses are becoming clearer. Spiritual qualities and faith are automatically awakened by pure intention, which at first seems to fasten to pure appearance, though actually it is concentrating toward openness. Then, as pure experience develops, we soar to the appearance of total openness. Finally, as our mind unfastens from appearances through the nonattachment that comes from vast emptiness, all appearances become the measureless, pure appearances of Buddhas. As Mipham Rinpoche, the Holy Triumphant One, said:

> By depending on the goal,
> The supremely born, goalless state is attained.

When the gross senses, joining with the gross habit of many lives, are drawn to a desirable object such as a beautiful song, if we do not transform them, they become deceiving enemies fooling us with the delusion of sadness or excitement. If we do transform them, they become truly undeceiving friends because they are the nonattached liberation of wisdom appearance.

Whenever the senses move toward objects, we must immediately turn our minds to awareness which is never deluded and, inhaling pure wisdom elements, be inseparable with deity and rest in stainless spaciousness.

Whatever we see, we think it is seen through the eyes, but actually it is seen through the power of unobstructed, stainless awareness mind.

Whatever we hear, we think it is heard through the ears, but actually it is heard through the power of unobstructed, stainless awareness mind.

Whatever we smell, we think it is smelled through the nose, but actually it is smelled through the power of unobstructed, stainless awareness mind.

Whatever we taste, we think it is tasted through the tongue, but actually it is tasted through the power of unobstructed, stainless awareness mind.

Whatever we feel, we think it is felt through touch, but actually it is felt through the power of unobstructed, stainless awareness mind.

Intuition means knowing from the mind without relying on the gross senses. Because nihilists do not believe in the continuity of mind through previous lives, which is the source of intuition, they do not understand that their intuitions come from their previously developed intuitive faculties which are dormant and then rekindled from time to time.

Intuition can be developed on a limited worldly level, such as psychic humans do, on the more extensive supernatural level of gods and demigods, or on the pristine, sublime level of Buddhas. The level of intuition depends on how deeply and clearly one uses the senses, on the previous development of concentration, and on the object and intensity of the aim which builds the habit of how the senses function. Whatever is aimed for can be attained. With a worldly aim, there will be a worldly result, and one's intuition will be faulty. Even if one can intuit more than ordinary people, it will not be so important because the aim and concentration are limited. With a supernatural aim, intuition and prescience can be developed far beyond an ordinary level. With the aim to attain enlightenment, by practicing clear samādhi, the senses become transparent and there is no duality to be seen. When beings become sublime, there is no longer intuition. There is just the flawless omniscience of enlightenment, which is knowing everything directly, unobstructedly, clearly, and simultaneously.

It may seem difficult to practice with deity visualization since the obscured senses of the habit of ignorance prevent us from seeing the deity. But logically, deity naturally exists, since mind is not only empty nothingness but also has phenomena. Through our ordinary senses, we twist these phenomena into worldly phenomena which can all be contained within the six realms of existence. Even if we do not perceive all of these realms and just consider our own ordinary phenomena, it is obvious that they torment us like demons. A demon is anything that tortures us and causes suffering, even though it sometimes may seem to cause temporary happiness. As long as we misuse phenomena with a wrong point of view and deluded senses, demons are everywhere, taking many aspects and creating the negative energy of jealousy, hatred, desire, greed, and ignorance. This negative energy exists because we are not transforming our demon-influenced habit into pure wisdom deity phenomena.

Since we cannot prevent phenomena from occurring, the only beneficial choice is to transform them into wisdom phenomena. The actual meaning of deity is desireless wisdom phenomena always abiding inseparably with stainless wisdom senses. There is no death, birth, or negativity in pure phenomena. There is only positive energy, which is the basis of deity, continuously benefitting with always unobstructed, compassionate, immeasurable, flawless exaltation. All sublime deities have countless aspects which can be synthesized into Nirmāṇakāya, Sambhogakāya, and Dharmakāya deities. Their aspects are always pure because their essence is always substanceless. Followers of the Vajrayāna path practice with deity visualization in order to recognize actual deity. Also, even though other doctrines do not teach about deity, if the state of enlightenment is reached, it is deity.

Because we do not recognize the light, unobstructed nature of our deathless wisdom body, the coarse karmic body and senses that we consider to be the self are formed. Then, our habit of only considering the energy of tangible gross substance to be true through the misinterpretation of obscured senses creates the repeating, deluded experience of birth and death, which is untrue. From karmic habit, the karmic senses continually change, ceasing and appearing again and again. When karmic senses vanish and phenomena cease, we think it is death, and when karmic senses arise and phenomena begin, we think it is birth.

If we only identify with the coarse energy of substance, we will have fear and misunderstanding. We will believe that death is true because we have no faith in our deathless nature, which is actual Buddha. Mind cannot be awakened by the influence of ordinary phenomena, which only strengthens our useless, old, samsaric habits. Mind must be awakened by invoking stainless Dharma appearance through deity. The invocation of deities frees us from habit because the nature of deities is naturally unobstructed light. We can only transform the habit of our coarse, heavy substance senses into light, boundless, wisdom senses through deity phenomena. By practicing, we can increase the wisdom qualities of our natural mind until our karmic cataracts are removed, and with our limitless wisdom eyes, we can see the infinite display of wisdom appearance.

Whenever the basis of mind and phenomena is free of all contrived, dualistic conception, it is absolute pure space, which is the basis of all pure phenomena. But as long as the basis of mind is unaffected by stainless wisdom, it is like a vast ocean which supports many deluded phenomena. Although the ocean's water is sometimes still, sometimes rippling, sometimes full of waves, and sometimes storming, none of these conditions can ever go beyond the quality of the ocean. The aspects of these phenomena change from different circumstances which arise through habit, but they never surpass being aspects of the ocean. In the same way, through the habit of delusion, sentient beings take each moment's waves seriously and believe they are permanent and real. Whenever the basis of ordinary mind remains obscured, we may think some phenomena are real and others are unreal, but all of these phenomena are deluded and never go beyond saṃsāra's recurring waves. Whenever we attain a precious human birth, we can have faith that Buddha nature can blossom through the pure reflection of Buddha Dharma and our own self-manifesting awareness mind. Through practice, we can recognize our wisdom mind, which releases us from continuous samsaric suffering to reach enlightenment. Buddha's enlightened wisdom mind is like stainless sky, inconceivable, untouchable, and uncatchable, which no one can affect or seed, and whose quality pervades everywhere unobstructedly.

Just as when there are no clouds in the sky and sunlight pervades everywhere, there are no divisions between the senses in Buddha's stainless wisdom mind. Wisdom mind is from the beginning perfectly self-accomplished wisdom senses. The wisdom senses of the Buddhas are always pure because the wisdom appearance of the Buddhas is only the reflection of the pure display of the wisdom light of sole awareness, which is the self-secret source of all maṇḍalas.

As it says in this precious, great treasure revealer's prayer:

Thus, whatever appearances arise as the object of the eyes,
All material phenomena of the outer container of the elements
      and inner essence of realms,
Even though they arise, just leave them in the natural state of
      nongrasping.
The object that is grasped and grasping mind are the pure,
      clear, empty body of the wisdom deity.
I pray to the lama of self-liberating desire,
I pray to Orgyen Padma Jungnay.

Thus, whatever sounds arise as the object of the ears,
All sounds, pleasant or unpleasant,
Just leave them in the natural state of empty sound free from
      thought.
Empty sound is neither born nor ceases; it is the speech of the
      Victorious Ones.
I pray to the empty sound of the speech of the Victorious Ones.
I pray to Orgyen Padma Jungnay.

Thus, whatever movement arises as the object of the mind,
Even though thoughts arise of the passion's five poisons,
Do not invoke, examine, or contrive by conception.
Just by leaving them as they are, they will be liberated into
    Dharmakāya.
I pray to the lama of self-liberating awareness,
I pray to Orgyen Padma Jungnay.

Karma

Alas! Saṃsāra is born from karma.
From karma, happiness and unhappiness
    are made.
Whenever conditions are gathered,
    they make karma,
And karma makes happiness and
    unhappiness again.

— LORD BUDDHA

There are many ways to understand the meaning of karma from different points of view within Buddhism. To synthesize some of these in a simple way, according to the point of view of the vehicle of cause, karma is the activity of cause and result. Within this vehicle, there are various explanations for the basis of karma. The Vaiśeṣika point of view teaches that karma originates in subjective consciousness; the Sutranta point of view teaches that karma originates in ordinary continuous mind; the Yogācāra point of view teaches that karma originates in the basis of all phenomena; and the Mādhyamika point of view teaches that karma originates in interdependent circumstances. In the context of practice, all points of view within the vehicle of cause teach that there is a basis for enlightenment, a path that leads to enlightenment, and a result of enlightenment.

According to the Vajrayāna point of view of the vehicle of result, it is unnecessary to divide cause from result or to consider that any activity follows from or leads to another activity. From the beginningless beginning, there is only the divisionless, pure nature of the maṇḍala of stainless Buddhas, and there are not even the names of cause and result. By recognizing this, all activity becomes the spontaneous display of Dharmakāya. With that point of view, we must abide in this recognition always, without the influence of the habit of ordinary mind's delusion, until we have complete confidence. But as long as we have dualistic mind, we divide cause from result and root circumstances from contributing circumstances. Through constantly making these divisions, we do not release saṃsāra's divided phenomena into nondualistic wisdom appearance. Instead, by grasping at appearances, we create duality, conceptions, passions, habits, and karma.

Because Buddha's speech is unobstructedly omniscient, it can be understood in many different ways according to the many different karmic capacities of beings in order to guide them to enlightenment, but however it is heard, it is meaningful. Since it is so rich and deep, each way of hearing it is true, and all can benefit from it according to their understanding. As it says in *The King of Sublime Samādhi Sūtra*:

> Buddha of universal benefit, even within your one word,
> Different sounds occur according to the wishes of different
> beings.
> Each one thinks, "The Victorious One is revealing this
> to me,"
> As you speak with a smile to anyone.

Only Buddhas do not have karma. All beings with dualistic mind are continually creating karma. There are many different methods according to different beings' capacities for purifying the karma of dualistic mind. Hīnayāna practitioners, through aversion to the suffering of saṃsāra, try to abandon the causes of karma, which are ego and the passions that arise from ego, in order to attain the enlightenment of self-peace. Mahāyāna practitioners try to realize that there is no possessor of a self and no possessor of phenomena, so therefore all phenomena become illusory with the freedom of nonattachment, which automatically opens immeasurable compassion toward beings

who do not realize this, in order to attain enlightenment for the benefit of countless beings. Vajrayāna practitioners, through the pure perception of deity appearance, try to transform all karmic phenomena
through nondualistic wisdom mind in order to attain enlightenment
in the immeasurable, pure maṇḍala of all Buddhas.

The idea of karma appeals to some people because it seems to
mean to them that they will not really die, but will reincarnate in
another form. But in Buddhism, it is pointless to just believe in the
continuity of ordinary mind without recognizing awareness mind.
Karma is created within dualistic mind, so it does not mean anything
to just accept that it exists if there is no understanding of how to be
released from karma and one does not even know where one will be
reborn. This kind of idea may cause more circling in dullness and
staying in saṃsāra. Just believing in a consciousness that continues
beyond death does not have any positive result without a wisdom
point of view of enlightenment. Although consciousness does not
die, it is not necessarily positive. For example, a ghost is not necessarily positive even though it represents consciousness beyond death.
Believing in an undying consciousness may not seem to be hopeless,
but actually, it has no hope if there is no idea of ultimate liberation.
As long as karma exists, we must try to change negative karma to
positive karma. This does not mean that karma is what we want, but
that we want to go beyond karma.

Although nihilists seem to accept the logic of the relation between cause and result, they are only considering the tangible and
perceptible causes and results within temporary, limited circumstances, which are only an extremely minor aspect of karma. They
do not acknowledge the intangible source of karma, which is the continuity of mind.

Only sublime beings such as Buddha know exactly how the previous karma of countless beings results in their karmic circumstances.
For ordinary beings, dualistic mind's heavy habit of dividing everything is like a wall that obscures the clear perception of the causes and
effects of karma. But through even a sprinkling of the nectar speech

of Buddha's stainless lotus lips on our ears, we can understand karma in a general way through reasoning.

According to the vehicle of cause, all activity creates karmic results. Until these results have ripened, karma cannot be changed by outer circumstances, just as a spring that has not yet exhausted itself cannot be stopped by covering it over with earth.

Karmic activity always comes from causes and goes to results. These results again create causes, just as when yogurt is added to fresh milk, new yogurt is made which can be used to make yogurt again. Depending on the yogurt's culture, it may have a bitter or sweet taste, just as intention which determines karmic results can be negative or positive.

Karma can be divided into the three categories of root circumstances, such as seeds; contributing circumstances, such as conditions for growth; and results, such as fruit. But since all future root circumstances come from results, just as seeds come from fruit, we cannot entirely separate root circumstances from results because they perpetually depend on each other. The only discrimination which can be made between them is according to changes of aspect that occur within dualistic mind's sequence of time. In order to increase our understanding, we can separate the stages of the karmic system according to the path of practice. But whether or not we know the relation between particular root circumstances and their results, it is possible for us to create new root circumstances from any result through intention.

The stages of karma are actually only relative to our point of view. To make a boat, the conception of the boat is the root circumstance, the materials needed to make the boat are the contributing circumstances, and the finished boat is the result. But if this boat inspires a plan to sail to another land, the completed boat would be a root circumstance. Within one event or form, the potential exists for both seed and result, just as within one ego, the potential exists for both saṃsāra and nirvāṇa. If the boat is not used, it may only be identified as a result because its relation to other circumstances is not recognized. In the same way, the implications of karmic relationships may not be seen due to our perspective, since we cannot be sure whether something is a cause or a result except within a particular context. Intangible causes are endlessly producing tangible results, and intangible results are endlessly arising from tangible causes.

The karma that arises is that which connects in time and place with temporary contributing circumstances. Just as the appearance of dream phenomena that are dormant in the mind are delayed until waking phenomena are exhausted, we should not expect, through our nihilist habit, that karmic results will always appear immediately after they are caused.

Karmic results may or may not ripen within the same lifetime in which they were created. Experiencing karma as obvious phenomena in the present is the result of karma caused in one life by negative or positive intention that ripens in that same life. Experiencing karma as obvious phenomena in the next life is the result of karma caused in one life that ripens in the following life, while other karmic results arise first. Experiencing karma as obvious phenomena in another, far future life is the result of karma that does not ripen in the present or following life, since its power remains dormant until other karmic results have been completed.

Karma is formed through the four conditions of basis, intention, application, and completion. In the example of aversion, the basis is the object of aversion, the intention is the wish to destroy the object, the application is the connection of the intention and the object in actually destroying the object, and the completion is the destruction of the object. In the example of attraction, the basis is the object of attraction, the intention is the wish to possess the object, the application is the connection of the intention and the object in actually possessing the object, and the completion is the possession of the object.

The gathering of the four conditions depends on the energy of the intention, and all four are necessary. For example, a painter needs an object such as paints as the basis of his activity. Even if he has the intention to paint, he will be unable to paint without this basis. If he has the basis of paints without the intention to do anything with them, the paints are unused. If there are both an intention to paint and the paints but still no activity of painting, there will not be an application. But when the application of the activity of painting connects with the painter's intention and with the basis of paints, the karma of completion occurs.

Karma always involves the interdependence of cause and result, which has five conditions. First, just as a seed ceases to exist when a plant grows from it, causes and results are not eternal. But also, secondly, a plant does not grow from the cause of a seed ceasing to exist. There is no exact moment that a seed ceases to exist and a plant's growth begins, because it is a gradual process in which one turns into the other. Just as there is a continuity of the transformation from a seed to a plant, so that a seed does not cease at a particular point, interdependent causes and results are not non-eternal. Third, the seeds and shoots of plants cannot be said to be the same as one another, since they have different aspects and processes. A seed cannot be said to be a shoot when it is only a seed, and a shoot cannot be said to be a seed when the shoot has grown. One cannot be said to be the same as the other, and one cannot be said to change from one into the other, because each is only a conceptual designation. All of the conceptual designations of the phenomena of causes and results are interconnected, but no certain connection can be made between them except at a relative level. Fourth, just as abundant fruit can come from a small seed, small causes can ripen into great results. Fifth, the kind of plant that will grow is determined by the kind of seed that is planted. For example, the seeds of wheat will not grow into other plants, but must become wheat. Just as when the seed of unvirtue is created, the result is unhappiness, and when the seed of virtue is created, the result is happiness, the correspondence between causes and results is unmistaken. These five conditions exist until the outer material of the elements, including beings' forms, and the inner elements of dualistic mind are exhausted in full enlightenment, which is beyond the interdependent causes and results of relative truth.

If the passions are not immediately dissolved through practice as they arise, their remaining influence will cause habits which cause karma. For example, if a person is bitten by a coiled snake and he experiences strong fear, this fear may return in the future if he sees a coiled rope because of his residual habit of fear. He will be caught between his deluded reality of snake and rope unless he can make his habit of fear disappear through practicing according to his capacity.

It is said in *The Treasure of Qualities*:

> The power of the various qualities of whatever seeds exist
> Is clearly shown to the farmers who have planted them.
> Likewise, the experiences of habits created over other lives
> Have caused the many different aspects of karma and the
> variations between sentient beings.

If we are attracted to objects which affect us, we must remember that it is not external reality which affects us, but only our previous habit of the reality of those objects reflecting back to us. As long as we have dualistic mind, we always think objects affect each other, but these effects are only the activity of habit created by the passions. For example, when we are awake, if we are attracted to someone through the habit of a previous karmic connection and create more habit through our attraction, we may begin to dream about this person. Also, just as our waking phenomena affect our dream phenomena, our dream attachment affects our waking phenomena. If we dream that we are separated from the person to whom we are attracted, we may awaken feeling sad, and if we dream we are united with this person, we may awaken feeling happy.

The strength of karmic effects depends on the strength of the passions formed by the mind's reflections and the energy of intention. For example, the winner of a game may be satisfied by winning, while the loser may think continuously about his frustrated desire to win. The loser, therefore, trains his mind with the energy of strong intention, which creates the new karmic form of the habit of winning. In a future game, the loser may conquer his opponent with the new energy he has created from his reaction to his previous defeat.

But samsaric losers and winners never realize that they are only play-
ing against their minds' apparitions, making what does not exist seem
to exist through the deluded power of habit.

As the karmic senses arise, if we have previously had a strong
habit of aversion, our disgust can arise easily through circumstances
as an effect of this habit. This disgust does not originate in these circumstances, but from our previous habit's projections, coming from
our mind and going to our mind. But we say our experience of this
negative feeling of aversion is caused by the object which is affecting
us. Then, with however much aversion we feel, we build our reaction
to our projection, creating the appearance of more and more form,
which we attach to the object of our projection. Even if we are separated from the tangible reality of the object, our disgust can return
through the strength of our previous aversion. Without recognizing
that our perception is a delusion, our aversion begins to exist even
without a tangible object, creating its own objects independent of the
original object, further separated from its source in mind. In this way,
new objects of aversion are automatically formed, creating a circle.
From time to time, from place to place, from life to life, habits are
formed again and again. Aversion is so deceiving; saṃsāra is so tiring.

As the karmic senses arise, if we have previously had a strong
habit of attraction, our desire can arise easily through circumstances
as an effect of this habit. This desire does not originate in these
circumstances, but from our previous habit's projections, coming
from our mind and going to our mind. But we say our experience of
this good feeling of attraction is caused by the object which is affecting us. Then, with however much attraction we feel, we build our
reaction to our projection, creating the appearance of more and more
form, which we attach to the object of our projection. Even if we are
separated from the tangible reality of the object, our desire can return
through the strength of our previous attraction. Without recognizing
that our perception is a delusion, our attraction begins to exist even
without a tangible object, creating its own objects independent of the
original object, further separated from its source in mind. In this

way, new objects of attraction are automatically formed, creating a circle. From time to time, from place to place, from life to life, habits are formed again and again. Attraction is so deceiving; saṃsāra is so tiring.

According to the vehicle of cause, when the state of Bodhisattva is attained, there is no reality of passions and no reality of karmic habits. However, the activity of Bodhisattvas still has the ability to influence beings who have karmic energy because of the power of the Bodhisattva's great accumulation and the prayers of complete dedication over many lives to benefit all sentient beings. Compassion naturally arises as stainless mind permeates phenomena. Since, for Bodhisattvas, all phenomena become like magic, they understand that sentient beings torture themselves by taking this illusory phenomena seriously. This great compassion spontaneously arises from the Bodhisattva's state of the afterglow of meditation, which is the state after the attainment of the stainless equanimity of nondualistic wisdom. According to the ordinary senses of sentient beings, Bodhisattva activity may seem to have an ordinary aspect, but this is only like an empty pot that may still have the faint, light fragrance of its former contents. Through continuously meditating, the compassion of Bodhisattvas becomes more aimless, and other beings are affected more strongly by it. Then, all habit disappears, without leaving even a trace. According to the inner vehicle of result, Bodhisattvas are enlightened the same as Buddha, and the Bodhisattva's aspect is only a form of Buddha's limitless emanations with many different activities. Since nondualistic wisdom mind is sole space, there is no object of compassion or subject that is compassionate. Compassion is the manifestation of the effortless, pure appearance of Nirmāṇakāya, inseparable from the naturally pervading, unobstructed, stainless sky space of Dharmakāya.

As long as our dualistic mind creates all negative, positive, short-lived, and long-lasting appearances which affect us through karmic energy, either while awake or while dreaming, we continually suffer from their lure and deception. If we want to be released from suffering, we must practice to dispel the effects of our passions, which cause our addiction to objects. Then we can change our blind attachment to saṃsāra's ensnaring objects through the blessing of the liberating words of Buddha.

In the sūtras, the example is given of a person who is sleeping in a jewel palace. Even though he is surrounded with beauty, he has horrible nightmares which he can only have because he is sleeping. There is also a person in the same jewel palace who is awake. He sees the person who is sleeping and tries to rouse him from his tormented dreams, exclaiming, "Your dreams are not true. We are in the same jewel palace, and if you awaken, there will be no nightmares." Like this, always unsleeping Buddha is always abiding in the jewel light of awareness mind. By not recognizing this light, sentient beings are in the dark sleep of unknowing, creating their samsaric misery. Buddha guides us toward his own pure appearances through his reflection of unobstructed wisdom so that all beings can awaken to the same measureless radiance.

By acknowledging that mind is continuous and the root circumstance of all phenomena, we must try to recognize its pure essence, which is Buddha nature. We must try to transform temporary obscurations into positive, contributing circumstances in order to become the same as all Buddhas. We must try to distill the pure essence from the unclear confusion of subject and object which remains in the fragile coincidence container of our nihilist habit's fragmented mind. Instead of creating impure and contradictory phenomena which are the cause of suffering, we must create pure and complementary phenomena through positive habits that create positive karma in our continuous Buddha nature land until we transcend the phenomena of relative truth and attain enlightenment.

It is unwise to disregard karma either through pretending to have a high point of view beyond karma or through nihilism, since it keeps us from trying to affect our karma through decreasing negative actions and increasing positive actions. Whether or not we believe in karma is itself a demonstration of the karma of our habit and conception. If we pay attention to karma, it will automatically strengthen our intention to create positive karma, and intention is the crux. Without strong intention, it does not matter what else is done, since it will not have any focus. That is why previous sublime saints have said:

> The difference between virtue and nonvirtue only
>   depends on intention,
> Not on the size of the form of virtue or nonvirtue.

One of the greatest nihilist misunderstandings is the mistaken belief that karma means our destiny is already decided and that we do not have control over our lives. Karma is misconceived by nihilists as just a support for unrealistic spiritual idealism, a fatalistic justification for life's difficulties, and an excuse for passivity.

Believing in karma does not mean that we should accept any circumstances and leave them as they are. In relation to ourselves, just as, if our hair and body caught on fire, we would try to extinguish the fire as quickly as we could, we must try to do whatever we can to be released from the karma of negative circumstances. In relation to others, just as a mother who sees her child drowning in a river would try to do as much as she could to rescue the child, belief in the karmic system implies that we think we can influence the destiny of others through intention and activity. The wish to try to prevent negative circumstances and suffering and to cause positive circumstances and happiness for all beings is important within the karmic system because it creates the seed of pure compassion and the right point of view. Any action taken in response to karmic situations is not only a reaction to previous karma, but creates the seed for future karma. Belief in the karmic system is not an excuse for accepting whatever happens, but an impetus for creating what we wish to happen.

Nihilists may believe that as much as we intend to cause a certain result, another result may occur unpredictably. In these cases, we may be unable to identify the connection between cause and result, and nihilists may use this to try to disprove karma. But actually, the reason that ordinary beings are unable to determine the exact connections of karmic causes and results is only due to their obscured and limited perception.

Whether or not we perceive it, dualistic mind always circles evenly back and forth among all phenomena, moving between many objects, between subject and object, between all negative and positive extremes, and between all causes and results. If we have elation, it will cause an equal amount of depression when the elation is exhausted. As Buddha said, it is tiring to live in saṃsāra because it is always circling evenly back and forth, and never releases toward one even goal.

Through our obstructed, short-sighted, nihilist, materializing calculations, we may think that karma is untrue because many beings are happy and enjoy good lives even though they do not believe in karma and do not think about nonvirtue and virtue or negative and positive intention, while others who do believe in karma and try with positive intention to abstain from nonvirtue and create virtue are suffering. But this is as unreasonable as saying that if the results cannot be immediately observed, any activity is useless. Whether or not sentient beings believe in or are aware of the consequences of their actions, they are always creating karma. When results cannot be foreseen or causes cannot be traced, it is only due to the limitations of miscalculated, nihilistic judgment and perception. Even when we try with intention to cause a particular result, another result may occur instead, which happens because of previous karmic effects that influence our circumstances. The causes and results that we notice are only temporary and conspicuous aspects of karma within samsaric time and place. But karma is not only occurring within these obvious circumstances that we notice. It is endless and continuous because ordinary mind, which creates karma, is endless and continuous.

If we do not believe in karma, we may believe that what we cannot understand is a mistake, an accident, or a coincidence, accepting illogical or unsystematic events and basic disorder. But within actual relative truth, it is only our misconceptions and the limitations of our perception which prevent us from seeing the connections between interdependent circumstances. Even when we think we perceive samsaric phenomena accurately through our own experience, it is also obvious through our own experience that we often misinterpret what we perceive and change our minds about what we think. Even when we think we are not misinterpreting what we perceive, we may later find that our new perceptions are only fresh misinterpretations. If there is no incisive point of view about how to be released from karma, everything is a mistake.

Even wars between countries can be created by the misconceptions of individuals whose karmic energy influences others through their karmic connection. Since the samsaric phenomena of relative truth depend on the misunderstandings, distorted perceptions, and misconceptions of countless beings, there is always confusion about the relation between the actual relative truth and inverted relative truth and between the general relative truth and personal relative truth of different beings, according to their individual and group karmic energy.

Even when beings think they understand each other, they have different understandings which are actually often misunderstandings. Within groups, between groups, and between themselves, beings are pulled toward and away from each other according to the strength of karma. But if karmic energy has not ripened, even though people are in the same place and would like to be connected with each other for either an ordinary or a spiritual purpose, they remain apart.

> There a mountain, here a mountain;
> They are seen by each other, but they never join.

Also, even though beings may not even know each other and have no wish to connect, when their karmic energy ripens, they come together.

> There a river, here a river;
> They are not seen by each other, but they join.

In this way, the different realities of different relative truths in the minds of different beings are always changing through the power of the karma that arises.

It is a habit of nihilism to say that when something positive happens, we caused it, and when something negative happens, it was an accident. We think we can avoid accidents, but if there is an accident, we think it was unavoidable. It is very strange that we believe in preventing what we believe we cannot prevent.

According to the Vajrayāna point of view, if we have pure intention and faith in the Triple Gems, we can change negative karma into positive karma by practicing with a determined mind and skillful means to transform ordinary karmic phenomena into wisdom activity.

If we believe in Buddha's stainless, nondualistic wisdom mind, even though various appearances arise, we will recognize that their essence has the same source. Although we can see many reflections in a mirror, the mirror itself has no inherent images. It only reflects the display of qualities through its potential to reflect. In the same way, there is only oneless one stainless space. It is only through the two extremes of nihilist or eternalist habit that we divide phenomena without recognizing the display of our mirror mind's reflections.

Through our divided mind's habit of separating cause and result, we may try to determine how particular actions affect karmic results by using our ordinary, dualistic thinking. But this is really just one more way that we disconnect the tangible from the intangible without recognizing their connection. With our habit of grasping, we constrict the undivided, light phenomena of Buddha's display, making it heavier and heavier, with more and more separation. This separating mind exists as long as we divide subject from object, which causes duality, grasping, and the defiled passions. Unless this separating mind is purified through practice, it circles between creating negative and positive karma.

Even if we try to purify karma, we may make the mistake of causing another impure activity within karmic phenomena. For instance, if we see a fault in ourselves and then change it, we may notice that former fault in others, becoming critical of them and self-righteous about ourselves. Only meditation can release us from holding and grasping and can let us actually know anything and everything with detachment and light. If we can meditate in stainless mind until we attain complete enlightenment, then there is no seed of karma. Meditation purifies the sediment of old habits and can prevent the cause of any new habits, just as it is impossible for dust to land in the clear flames of a fire since the fire immediately consumes it.

Nondualistic mind is unobstructed like a clean, clear mirror which never conceptualizes about the qualities of its reflections. Since Dharmakāya is unobstructed, stainless space, inexhaustible qualities of display can arise, such as the wrathful and peaceful appearances of wisdom deity phenomena. Pure discerning wisdom never causes delusion through discrimination between the aspects of appearance. But from our lack of recognition, we distinguish between negative and positive phenomena, dividing wrathful appearances from peaceful appearances and creating aversion and attraction toward phenomena. All Buddhas are self-sustaining within this display, without discriminating between its immeasurable aspects which have the same stainless essence.

According to Buddhism, existence means everything that is possible. Existence is not just this world's existence or the existence of this universe, but infinite existence, since sentient beings' conceptions, which create all that exists, are infinite. Buddhas' purelands of measureless wisdom display are also limitless. But through dualistic habit, we only believe in the existence of our perceptions and conceptions within the dualistic phenomena of inverted relative truth to be used for temporary benefit within saṃsāra. Whatever is momentarily found is taken seriously, but anything found with the limited consciousness and senses of ordinary mind cannot be ultimate.

There is no karma without relative truth, since the karmic system exists within the duality of relative truth. As long as the phenomena of relative truth exist, the truth of karma exists. As Atīśa said:

> There is no end to karma until dualistic conceptions are
> exhausted,
> So therefore, you must believe in the result of cause.

In the Hīnayāna and general Mahāyāna perspectives, the karmic system is accepted as the support of relative truth's phenomena in order to encourage beings to purify obscurations and accumulate merit until they attain enlightenment. It is a reflection that adapts to those who would deny the validity of relative truth and karma without having confidence in vast, nondualistic wisdom mind, a mistake which only results in their turning toward chaotic nihilism and being discouraged from taking the path toward enlightenment.

Whatever path we take to transcend dualistic mind, karma cannot be denied until we recognize and abide in the stainless nature of wisdom mind, which is beyond karma. According to their karmic habit, Buddhist practitioners choose to abandon the phenomena of ordinary reality by having faith and practicing on the path of their karmic habit's connection. They do this with the Hīnayāna point of view that teaches how to destroy one's own passions, which are the cause of samsaric suffering, through the realization of selflessness; with the Mahāyāna point of view which teaches that all sentient beings have essential Buddha nature and that with nonattachment, phenomena can be recognized as unreal and illusory; and with the Vajrayāna point of view which teaches that all sentient beings are beginninglessly Buddha and that the phenomena of ordinary reality can be transformed into the pure deity display of all Buddhas' appearances.

Everything within time and place is relative. What is intangible causes what is tangible, and what is tangible causes what is intangible. Whatever is considered to be ultimate is momentary because interdependent circumstances are momentary and never appear all at once. Whenever they start to appear, they start to change. Anything that we try to decide is definite within relative truth is uncertain, since it always depends on our relative perspective. Even if we try to determine a particular cause, we will not be able to determine a certain result for it. Whatever we decide is its result will only be one possibility which we have chosen from our own point of view. From every point of view that is taken, there is another potential result. Actually, there is no certain cause. We just create what we think is a certain cause, and a certain result seems to come through our habit.

Samsaric phenomena only appear because of the habit of our

obscurations. Yet according to the Vajrayāna point of view, even our obscurations do not originally exist. It is only that since everything can appear, anything can exist and does exist. Since sentient beings do not realize Vajrayāna's point of view, they grasp at these appearances so that cause and result appear and samsaric phenomena appear as connected, continuous, interdependent circumstances.

Stainless wisdom mind is the unending openness of no cause, no result, no time, and no place. But as long as we are obscured from this recognition through habit and we exist within time and place, karma exists.

Since the essence of karma is that it is an appearance within time and place, the determination of relative causes and results depends on knowing the circumstances of time and place. But even if we thought that it was possible to make these determinations, there would be no way to know everything exactly without understanding all general and personal phenomena with unobstructed wisdom senses.

According to circumstances, sometimes a certain cause can seem to lead to a certain result, and sometimes the relation between cause and result may seem indefinite or unpredictable. But by accepting the truth of cause and result, we do not need to think that the cause and result are always tangible. Whether or not we think we can determine a particular cause or result depends on whether or not the circumstances have appeared for their observation. As Fearless Great Islander, Rigdzin Jigmed Lingpa, said:

> As birds glide high above the ground,
> Even though their shadow is not seen for a while,
> Since, unavoidably, a body cannot separate from its shadow,
> Whenever circumstances ripen and the bird lands, its shadow
>   becomes obviously apparent.

Whether a particular event is itself a cause or a result cannot be answered except in relation to circumstances. Since subtle circumstances are within gross circumstances and gross circumstances are within subtle circumstances, it is unnecessary for us to always analyze them; either can be the other, and circumstances are always changing. An observer with ordinary mind has no power to predict or to produce a certain effect on circumstances that have not yet ripened. Only sublime beings can know how circumstances are related.

If we do not believe in something, it automatically means that we believe in something else. It is unnecessary to think that a particular cause always has to appear to us in order to be connected with a particular result. Appearance causes nonappearance, and nonappearance causes appearance.

The nihilist habit is to believe what is observed, so there is a great interest in knowing the relation between particular causes and particular results. But since according to Buddhism, anything can exist, observers and their observations only locate and name particular aspects of infinite phenomena.

Everything is uncertain and depends on our perspective because everything within relative truth is interdependent. When circumstances arise and are apparent, we call them results, and when circumstances are dormant and subtle, we call them causes. For general phenomena, cause comes before result. But actually, cause creates result and result creates cause. Their order only comes from ordinary beings and depends on ordinary beings' misunderstanding, understanding, misinterpretation, and interpretation of phenomena. There is no intrinsic order.

The illusory characterization of phenomena occurs when sentient beings perceive and name sudden, temporary phenomena with dualistic conception. When phenomena are transformed through practice and become wisdom display, they are the appearances of undeluded realization. As Vajrayāna teaches, we must change our ordinary, deluded reality's identification of phenomena by practicing and creating positive habit until becoming habitless Buddha.

Whatever is said is just the name of an illusory characterization of phenomena. According to relative truth, it could be said that there is a connection between objects and names. For example, people answer when their names are called. But according to absolute truth, there is actually no connection between anything and any name. If we try to find an essence of a name, we cannot find either an essence of a name or of an object to name, so there is no connection between them. If there is no connection between them, no interdependent circumstances are created. As it is said in *The King of Sublime Samādhi Sūtra*:

> Whenever a child is born,
> Someone gives him a name of this or that.
> But if one searches for that name, it cannot be found
>   anywhere.
> It must be found that all phenomena are like that.

In general, in order to benefit others, it is important to try to make connections between the ideas of other perspectives and the Buddhist point of view. But there is a basic difference between non-Buddhist ideas, which always contain a strong habit of believing in reality, and Buddhist ideas, which try to make all of what seems to be real into what is unreal. It is difficult for non-Buddhists to understand Buddhist ideas easily because of this strong habit of reality. Like the difference in perspectives between a child and a wise man in a discussion about rainbows, even when the same image is considered, each observer has a different reaction due to his different understanding.

According to general Buddhism, all ideas are unreal, but to increase the untouchable essence that ideas only try to catch, the illusory characterizations of phenomena are used to increase inconceivable, positive phenomena and positive habit in a vast, long-lasting way to open the path to enlightenment. Ordinary, illusory characterizations of phenomena do not come from wisdom, but from habit. We are afraid to stop thinking about the reality through which these unreal characterizations are created. But fear is only loyalty to habit. By recognizing the unreality of our phenomena, we can change them into the positive appearances of the positive path leading to the result of the great, beginningless freedom of space.

Within interdependent circumstances, whether cause and result are considered to be uncertain possibilities or whether they seem to be momentarily connected and certain does not prove anything. Both interpretations come from deluded mind and are only expressions of ordinary, illusory characterizations of phenomena. Everything is uncertain within samsaric phenomena, including the circumstances of cause and result.

There is not any final reality within temporary circumstances. We may understand that something may occur and call it a possibility, but there is no actual possibility. If there is a conception of a possibility, a possibility may arise, but there is no way to determine what is possible or what is definite within dualistic mind. Because of effects that seem to occur with no cause or because of causes with unpredictable results, we may decide with our ordinary mind that there is no time and no place so that there is no cause and result. But this naming of no time and no place is itself a basic time and basic place in which cause and effect are dormant. These names of timelessness and placelessness are only ideas within the unbalanced energy of dualistic mind's ordinary disorder that cannot be compared to timeless, placeless, unobstructed, and inconceivable enlightened mind.

If we think that something actually exists, it already means that it does not exist. It exists only from our habit. Whatever we conceive of as existing always vanishes, always diminishes, is always exhausted, and is always destroyed. It is just that we name each habit, as we could name a horn of a rabbit.

There is no real existence of anything other than habit. No matter what we find, it is always false and will be the beginning of what cannot be found. But because we have temporarily identified our deluded phenomena with a name through the habit of time and place, we think that we have found something.

As it has been said by sublime saints of ancient times, if someone who is childless dreams that her son has died, this is delusion. If when she awakens she thinks that she has no son and no one has died, it is still delusion. The only difference is between the illusory times and places of habit, which always finds what is untrue and true, although neither are true.

Sentient beings suffer because of their reality, thinking of reality, creating reality, and always wandering in frustration between realities. When we create reality, unreality automatically comes, and we go back and forth between real and unreal.

Through karmic habit, sentient beings remain in a cycle of inverted phenomena created by inverted perceptions, like a circle of fire appearing to a child watching a whirling torch. When inverted appearances are seen with uninverted perception, it is like an adult knowing that the circle of fire is not what it seems. Sublime beings who have wisdom mind see uninverted appearance with uninverted perception, so perception and appearance become the pure reflection of display.

To change karmic habits, we must change our perception so that instead of continually being caught by our creations of distorted phenomena, we can transform our perception through creating pure phenomena to go beyond all inverted perception and appearance, which is stainless Buddha.

In all of the causal vehicle's traditions, karma is continuous until enlightenment is attained. The only difference is in whether negative or positive karma is caused, which depends on individual intention and activity. According to the Mahāyāna teachings, Buddha nature is the cause and enlightenment is the result. In the Vajrayāna tradition, Buddha nature is not discussed. To attain enlightenment, one has to acknowledge beginningless, primordially complete Buddha. There is no result different from this purity, since this purity always pervades from the beginning and is inseparable from the result of enlightenment. There is no division between relative and absolute truth, which is indistinguishable sublime truth.

Although the sun itself is completely pure, it may momentarily be obscured by clouds. In order to recognize and abide in the sunlight of our beginningless purity, we must dispel the clouds of our habits and separate from temporary obscurations. In order to do this, the activities of the stages of visualization and meditation are practiced, but these do not cause saṃsāra. They only cleanse the tarnish of temporary obscurations from beginningless purity, as wind cleanses clouds from the sun. The sun is the sun already, so it is not necessary to try to cause another new sun's shining. Serious Vajrayāna practitioners with devotion can learn about this from highly realized teachers and thoroughly establish this point of view without misinterpretation for the benefit of building ego. Just as the sun shines, we are free from the beginning. Just as the sun will not be a different sun when clouds are gone, enlightenment is the attainment of the original purity.

As long as sentient beings remain within karmic time and place, they will wander between the lower and higher realms of samsaric phenomena. By understanding and believing in karma, we can have the great intention to create positive conceptions, habits, and karma so that through transcending karmic time and place, we abide in Buddha's appearance.

As Buddha said, "You can have rebirth in higher or god realms, but without the intention to reach enlightenment, you cannot reach enlightenment. But with intention, you can definitely reach enlightenment." That is why Nāgārjuna made the wish for Bliss Sustaining King in *Message to a Friend*:

> Some beings go from dark to dark,
> Some from dark to light,
> And some from light to dark.
> May you go from light to light.

Love and Faith

For those of you who want to attain enlightenment, do not study many teachings. Only
study one. What is it? It is great compassion.
Whoever has great compassion has all Buddha's qualities in his hand.

— LORD BUDDHA

In the undeluded purity of self-appearance, there are no names of love
and faith, because there is no reality of an object of sentient beings
and no substantiality of an object of deities. But since all sentient
beings grasp at the uncatchable display of appearance, all our phenomena become heavy and substantial, and we create the duality of
self and other, the conceptions of ordinary mind, and the karmic
delusion of habit. Since all habit belongs to either the deluded panic
of saṃsāra or the noble path of enlightenment, it is best to develop
the positive habit of the path of enlightenment that always creates the
positive energy of love and faith, until we attain the selfless appearance of the Buddhas.

Love and faith have the same essence of deep caring. The only
difference is that love is aimed toward sentient beings, including those
who are less fortunate than we are, and faith is aimed toward sublime
beings, including all Buddhas and enlightened guides. The nature of
love is to give positive energy to others in order to benefit them and
to release them from suffering. The nature of faith is to trust in sublime beings in order to receive the blessings of wisdom energy that

benefit oneself and others. True faith creates the vast love of compassion that benefits countless beings.

If we rely on ordinary, dualistic mind, we cannot have deep and lasting love either for our equals or for less fortunate beings, because ordinary, dualistic mind depends on the uncertainty of temporary circumstances. This uncertainty easily causes disinterest, hatred, or betrayal. If we do not believe in the unending continuity of mind, we will only consider the immediate, tangible circumstances of our connections to others, rejecting or accepting them as these circumstances change according to what is the most expedient for us. Ordinary love that arises from the karmic results of habit can seem to have the qualities of being genuine, loyal, and stable, but these qualities only mask the potential for the opposite qualities of insincerity, disloyalty, and instability to arise if circumstances change. Because ordinary love has no depth, it is automatically limited. If it becomes unpleasant, we stop feeling it. When we only react to circumstances, we are really just considering ourselves and our own reactions without respecting or caring deeply about others. When we feel isolated and want to be loved, we show love to others in order to receive love from them in return, but when we are satisfied, we forget about others. This is not enduring and continuous love. It does not cause the impartial compassion of Bodhisattvas because it depends on our personal, selfish desire.

If we do not believe in anything beyond what can be experienced directly with the obscured perception of dualistic mind, we will not recognize that our awareness is limited and we will only care about our immediate experiences. Our main interest will be in our own temporary benefit, even though this benefit is easily lost because it depends on unreliable, temporary circumstances.

If we only react with self-interest to whatever circumstances appear, we will make choices based on trying to find temporary satisfaction. But this effort is always ultimately hopeless, since everything within saṃsāra is uncertain because it is changing. Through the shortsightedness of our habit, we do not even notice that we are missing what is meaningful, like someone who eagerly chooses to eat a cow's red meat instead of continuously drinking its white milk.

If we believe that mind is continuous, our love for others becomes continuous. If we recognize this continuity, we do not trust temporary, tangible circumstances or take them too seriously. Since it is tiring to switch between changing uncertainties which are inherently impermanent and unimportant, we become less easily influenced by any circumstance. This creates the habit of stability so that our minds are less erratic, our lives are less chaotic, and our feelings for others are less changeable, which causes love to become increasingly deep and loyal.

If we believe in the continuity of mind, then love inconspicuously connects us to the ones we love with continuous positive energy, so that even tangible separations between people who love each other do not reduce the intangible power of love. This love is automatically enduring since it is not easily affected by circumstances.

If we can keep from grasping at others with the selfish fear of losing them or the hope of possessing them through the unawareness of our ordinary, dualistic mind, then the energy of love increases and its quality of giving energy to others opens and expands. The positive habit of continuity is created by not depending on what occurs each moment as though it were the only moment. By believing in the continuity of mind, we acknowledge the continuity of all circumstances, including our experiences of love, which are not just for one moment or for one life. We can understand that it is useless to try to escape from momentary dissatisfaction or to pursue momentary benefit by abandoning old circumstances and chasing after new circumstances, since nothing really changes unless we are released from all circumstances to enlightenment.

Through our nihilist habit, we may superficially judge the relationships between parents and children, friends and companions, or teachers and students, deciding that they are inharmonious or unsuitable. If we do not believe in continuous mind and continuing karmic connections but only believe in coincidental circumstances, we may think that it is better to discard difficult relationships in order to rid ourselves of problems, and we may easily turn away from others.

But if we believe in continuous mind and karma, we know that momentary phenomena always change. Unless change is connected with practice leading to enlightenment, it is unnecessary to try to change our useless, worldly phenomena, which only takes us from being miserable to being miserable again. We will not take temporary negativity so seriously if we know that all circumstances within gross and subtle substantial conceptualization are impermanent. We will also not want to hold onto negative feelings that increase negative habits, since we will recognize that there is no benefit in doing this. By believing that we can actually change our karmic circumstances, we can pray for others, purify negativity, and create positive karma with the intention of attaining enlightenment. Instead of trying to change our outer circumstances, we will understand that it is more meaningful to change our own phenomena.

In order to increase the measureless, positive presence of the pure appearance of wisdom, our connections to others should always be joined to Dharma. Unlike the temporary aim and duration of ordinary love, our love for others can be for ultimate benefit. The intention of love can be the same as the intention of faith, to lead to enlightenment, which releases us from the suffering of worldly, superficial love. We can create this basic motivation for all of our connections to others. We can also aspire to follow the Bodhisattvas who, through great compassionate love for others, vow to empty saṃsāra. As it is said, "Until the miserable wailing of the suffering of all beings ceases, the illness of the Bodhisattva is never cured."

As long as we are dying and being born within saṃsāra, it is important to pray for a human birth through which we can connect to Dharma. Even for nihilists, humans are considered superior to other beings because of their intelligence. The source of this intelligence is continuous mind, from which infinite appearances can arise, from the phenomena of ordinary human beings to the appearances of enlightenment. By the aspiration to be born as a human being with parents who believe in Dharma, we try to create positive circumstances through family love and to increase faith that will continue from life to life. Also, it is important for parents, teachers, and others who are more experienced to cultivate a noble Dharma habit in their children, students, and others who are inexperienced, in order to create a link with Buddha's speech.

Except for beings who are born without the circumstance of parents, such as beings born through the elements of heat and moisture, beings born through habit in the hell realms, or many sublime beings born without habit through miraculous wisdom, including Padmasambhava, all beings are born through parents who give love to their children. First, we must acknowledge this love and try to love all sentient beings, who have been our parents over countless lives. Second, it is not enough to just think of their kindness to us; we must give tremendous kindness to them. Third, if they have positive qualities and their lives are happy, we must rejoice instead of being jealous. Fourth, we must be loving, kind, and rejoice for all beings equally. These are the four boundless wishes.

Most people become preoccupied with their attachments to others without ever using the opportunity of human birth to open their minds. They keep their habit of grasping at others for their own satisfaction and continually switch between momentary unhappiness and happiness.

Instead of connecting to ordinary objects which are temporary and may cause negativity, it is better to visualize, have faith in, or even just think of Buddhas, and be with them inseparably. They are the unchangeable companions and greatest comforters.

The only difference between saṃsāra and enlightenment is attachment. We can even turn whatever experiences come through practice into worldly phenomena if we become attached to them. On the other hand, even though we may appear to be involved in worldly activities, if we have recognized that all phenomena are the unattached, free, and open appearance of awareness, everything is liberated.

The antidote for attachment is to know that all phenomena are substanceless and immaterial. It is not that we are just making up an idea of emptiness and imposing it on phenomena, but that phenomena are naturally empty. Emptiness cannot be grasped. The essence is that there is no form of graspable substance. There is only stainless emptiness. There is also not nothingness, because empty form is the luminous, completely light, exaltation form of deity, which is totally different from heavy, karmic form. Seeing this luminosity of appearance releases us from ordinary attachment and dullness.

Just as we can use any samsaric phenomenon to create new phenomena, through practice we can transform the ordinary attachment of love into the positive appearances of deity. In this way, the energy of the passions of ordinary love can be used with faith to increase wisdom qualities so that we can attain enlightenment. When the attachment of ordinary love and ordinary passions is changed through practice into the attachment to sublime phenomena and sublime qualities, self-seeking love can become the extraordinary love of seeking selflessness. As the pure appearances of deity practice increase wisdom qualities, and the emptiness of meditation releases us from attachment to these appearances by seeing the immaculate, empty essence of deity, the inseparability of inexhaustible, unobstructed phenomena and great oneness opens.

As long as our minds are deluded, anything can seem true to us, including our ordinary passions as they occur in our attachments to others. By creating substantial conceptions and forms, and thinking that they are true, we grasp at them and create all samsaric phenomena. But whatever we name as true becomes untrue.

Wherever there are samsaric phenomena, there is enlightenment; we only have to change our ordinary phenomena into wisdom appearance. If we can believe, practice, and accomplish the essence of the Vajrayāna samaya of pure phenomena, then everything is deity. When there is no more grasping at conception, complete, unobstructed illumination manifests. So instead of grasping, we must be released into light.

If we rely on ordinary, dualistic mind, we cannot have deep and enduring faith, because whenever circumstances change, our faith can easily change so that we give up our beliefs. If we experience a feeling of faith, we want to believe in something, but what we really believe in is only whatever appears in front of us for the moment. Whenever this temporary experience decreases, we disregard what we believed in and discard our faith.

If we only believe in the tangible phenomena of temporary circumstances because of attachment to substance, we will not be able to recognize the profound, intangible qualities of wisdom mind. This is because we believe strongly in the truth of our own deluded perceptions and we disbelieve what we cannot perceive. As long as we do not believe in vast wisdom qualities, we will stay trapped in our disbelief and we will not try to increase intangible, light phenomena which always give positive energy and encourage us to transform our ordinary phenomena.

Even though the moon shines in the sky with clear light, unclear water cannot reflect it. Even though wisdom mind has inconceivable qualities in which we can have faith, we cannot recognize them if we only believe in the obstructed perceptions of ordinary, dualistic, fragmented mind. If we cannot reflect the vast qualities of wisdom mind, we will not be able to recognize the nature of these qualities or find them within ourselves. If we only have pessimistic disbelief, the qualities of disbelief and pessimism will arise. Sometimes we meet beings who have created such unpleasant, abrasive energy that we cannot understand how to be with them for even one minute. They have this uncomplementary energy because they have been disconnected from pure, spiritual love and faith for many lives, so others reject them because of their heaviness or aggression.

There are many methods for increasing positive energy, but the most powerful of these is to create love and faith which arise from original, intangible wisdom energy. If we connect through faith to the vast, profound continuity of mind, the deep, smooth, soothing, light qualities of wisdom energy can flower. The essence of love is the compassion of sublime beings which always gives energy with inconceivable, positive qualities. Those who have been blessed by the wisdom energy of sublime beings for many lives have energy that enlivens and refreshes others. Just seeing these people has a positive effect. When there is a deep connection, the effect is immeasurable. According to history, even when Bodhisattvas were captured and held by enemies, they were happy and relaxed as a sign of their positive, loving energy which remained open and giving.

If we do not have faith at the time of death, we are like innocent, helpless animals because of attachment to material existence, even though all material, including our karmic bodies, inevitably becomes immaterial. We will be targetless, with fear as our only companion. When we grow old, we may at best try to find a friend who is as pathetic and powerless as we are due to not having the gentle nectar rain of the blessings of sublime beings. If we only rely on others to affect our energy for our temporary satisfaction instead of trying to increase inner energy, we will never stop depending on outer circumstances, which are always unreliable and changeable. Because of our nihilist habit, we usually do not want to even hear anything about death. Because of our fear, we try to avoid it through the dullness of not thinking about it. Without faith, we cannot be fearless about death, since true fearlessness comes from faith.

Because of previous karmic habit, even if we do not recognize that Buddhas are not separate or different from us, we can still develop positive habits by believing in them and praying to them with deep faith, which brings positive energy. If we think of Buddhas as the most comforting companions whom we can visualize and pray to according to the tradition we follow, at least we are not relying on fragile, impermanent samsaric phenomena. We are nurturing the seed of enlightenment. But if we are only distracted by trying to catch a tangible, external deity, as though deity were an object, without recognizing the intangible, dormant deity of our own mind, we will not catch the profound meaning of actual deity.

From the Buddhist point of view, deity is never disconnected from our own pure mind. In order to change ordinary habit to enlightened mind, Buddhists invoke the vision of an external deity in practice, always believing that this deity is indivisible from the deity of their own wisdom Buddha mind. This is the point of view in all Buddhist deity practices, in which the deity and the practitioner become inseparable. When we attain the fearless confidence that Buddhas are reflections of our own wisdom mind, there is no difference between outer and inner phenomena and no division between external and internal deity, since mind is free of duality and is like sky. Believing this, we must find Buddha through our own practice, and we must practice with faith until outer and inner appearance become indivisible.

Whether the omniscient Buddhas appear in desireless form, such as in the aspect of Buddha Śakyamuni in monk's robes, or in desirable form, such as in the aspect of Vajrasattva in union with his consort and Padmasambhava with many wisdom consorts and surrounding retinue, these appearances are never caused by dualistic mind. They manifest from the stainless space of Dharmakāya, just as a mirror's reflections come from its unobscured power to reflect perfectly and unobstructedly. The inconceivable qualities of the Buddhas cannot even be imagined by beings with gross elements and gross conceptions. But through the connection of sublime teachings and methods, the appearances of the Buddhas can be recognized as never different from our own essential nature.

If we believe in the continuity of mind, we are released from the habit of pessimism. Then, through the optimism of faith, we can create positive karmic conditions to experience the phenomena of the higher realms, to take a precious human birth, or to be transformed into deity in pureland. We can also have faith that our sublime guides can release us from this life's suffering. According to actual relative truth, we may think that sublime beings want us to become enlightened. Within the causal vehicle, this is true for Bodhisattvas who have the vast intention to act impartially for the benefit of all beings. But there is no intention in the complete enlightenment of the vehicle of result, so there is no difference between Bodhisattvas and

Buddhas, who always abide in nondualistic, immeasurable Buddha-field phenomena. At the same time, benefit just comes naturally for the phenomena of other beings, without intention and with unobstructed compassion. Even our perception of the appearance of pure activity is only our way of connecting to the effortless blessings of the Buddhas.

Due to having been nihilists continuously for many lives, and due to imposing the belief in political and social equality of this degenerate age onto a spiritual level, many people cannot accept the idea of having faith in others. Because of their own ego, this idea causes the threatening conception that others are better than they are. Even though they say they believe in the idea of equality for others, their distaste for the conception of the superiority of others actually means that they do not want to feel unequal themselves. What makes this ridiculous is that even if they hold these ideas strongly, there is always an unavoidably unequal condition between all beings. That is why there is always conflict and there has never been and will never be evenness in the general scenery of this world.

Having faith is especially difficult for intellectuals who study either worldly or spiritual systems of thought for the purpose of building their ordinary ego's reputation, with the ambition of developing this life's ideas. They cannot receive blessings because they are only adding to their ordinary ego and solidifying negative energy. That is why it has been said in tantric teachings:

> Whoever is wise about the true meaning of the nature
>   of appearance,
> That wise person is close to attaining siddhi.
> Or, whoever has stable faith with a simple mind,
> That person is close to attaining siddhi.
> Whoever thinks and conceptualizes,
> That person is far away from attaining siddhi.

The meaning of faith is to see qualities in others that are much more wonderful than and superior to one's own. There are three kinds of faith: the faith without reason that makes the mind clear, like an innocent child who is delighted with pure phenomena inside a beautiful temple; the faith of desire to receive superior qualities; and the faith of complete belief in sublime beings without doubt, so that one can receive their blessings and become the same as they are. In order to recognize our own wisdom qualities, we must depend on outer positive circumstances, which in this case means meeting those who can show the correct way to do this. Without faith or guidance, it is impossible to know how to do this in the right way. We must have faith in order to open the quality of our own Buddha nature. Through having faith in teachers who show us the correct way until we have full confidence, the outer object of faith joins with our own inner Buddha.

Many nihilists think that if someone who was previously a nihilist takes refuge in Buddha, he must have been brainwashed. They feel that Buddhism has had too much of an influence on his mind since his phenomena are no longer complementary to their own. Particularly if they think he is changing as a result of his practice, they see it as proof of brainwashing, without considering how everything and everyone are always changing constantly and unavoidably, both noticeably and unnoticeably. From the Buddhist perspective, the purpose of practice is to change one's deluded, dualistic phenomena. It may be a positive sign if someone changes, if he actually decreases ordinary ego and attachment to ordinary power in this life without being contrived or hypocritical, and increases wisdom energy for unending benefit. Actually, all of the phenomena of sentient beings within karmic habit and conception are brainwashing. It is only the content of the brainwashing that is different. When we decide to rely on the Buddhist wisdom methods of using the mind to change the mind, it is not brainwashing with a wrong, worldly point of view; it is cleansing the mind with the nectar of the wisdom point of view, going beyond karmic habit by changing our ordinary phenomena to the pure appearance of wisdom.

If we do not have faith and are only curious about spiritual ideas from a cultural point of view, we can become callous and insensitive to profound teachings without ever actually understanding them. Whatever is learned can seem to become familiar and stale if it is disconnected from the unimaginable manifestation of pure wisdom energy. What is learned from practice causes unshakable faith and is always uncontrived. But if we only have curiosity without faith, we will not be as interested in actual practice as we will be in acquiring other people's ideas, which just add to our own fragmented and inert conceptions. Even if we are receiving, studying, learning, and thinking about teachings, we will not have positive, spiritual experience without having faith and without practicing them. Through thinking that we know more than others, there is only the danger of building the extreme arrogance of a false scholar's ego. Whatever is known by an ordinary, intellectual mind is changing and will be exhausted because it is changing. Ordinary ideas that are disconnected from wisdom mind cannot illuminate unending knowledge. Without a vast point of view, even ideas about Dharma can be misused to support our samsaric ego. In this way, even spiritual qualities can easily turn into their opposite. It is very difficult to have actual faith.

For ordinary beings, knowledge causes cognitive obscurations by creating attachment to what is known, obstructing the perception of limitless other phenomena through this adherence to a particular focus. But if we practice with faith, ego can be purified through the detachment that comes from knowing that all circumstances are illusory. This releases us from all attachment, so that we are never trapped in a particular place which would obscure our perception of other places. Nothing can affect us because everything is the display of wisdom, which is the source of indivisible, sublime, natural faith.

It is not only knowledge that can be misused. Some practitioners also misuse the experiences of practice in this way. Instead of releasing attachment to their experiences through vast, spacious emptiness, they cling obsessively to their experiences with their ordinary ego and increase self-righteousness, creating a false saint's ego. The wisdom of unobstructed, unattached knowing comes through the blessing of the source of faith, which is practicing in a simple way without being lost in many fabricated ideas. This does not cause cognitive obscurations because it has no attachment. Attachment is the seed of all obscurations.

Even if we cannot recognize wisdom qualities due to the karmic obscuration of our belief in tangible reality, we must still decide that this is only because we are not perceiving what is actually there. We must believe strongly that even though we seem to be disconnected, we can connect. When we are in darkness, we have to go toward the lamp to light it, and then the lamplight shines back on us. We must use effort, since even faith depends on intention. With faith, we can unveil the essence of Dharma.

If we have faith in sublime beings, we automatically want to hear more and more about their qualities. Through hearing more and more, we will be influenced by their qualities and try to follow their examples, which show us how we can increase only the positive, infinite, light qualities of wisdom mind. Just as rain restores and increases a river, it is necessary to have faith to increase pure, natural qualities to be the same as Buddha.

Whoever has the intention to attain enlightenment for the benefit of all beings must have faith, following the ten examples of faith given in the sūtras by Buddha Śakyamuni: never tired, like a bridge that carries many burdens without complaining; never sad, like a ship that does not say its load is too heavy; never changing from any circumstances, like a mountain; never decreasing or increasing, like the quality of the sun, and so on. Otherwise, as Buddha Śakyamuni said:

> People who do not have faith
> Cannot have white Dharma,
> Just as a seed burned by fire
> Cannot sprout a green shoot.

The intention to have faith creates faith. A clear intention is extremely important in all Dharma because it focuses energy and defines our aim so that we can attain it. Without intention, energy is wasted, diffused, and lost, preventing any accomplishment. If we have the strong intention to practice in order to reach enlightenment, we can dedicate all of our activity toward this intention.

As much as our intention is limited, the result will be limited. If we have a vast intention, no one can prevent its fulfillment because of the unpreventable strength of natural mind. This is obviously known from the activity of sublime beings. If we wish to help and serve others through love, and to become the same as sublime beings through faith by praying and offering to them, without expecting immediate, substantial rewards, one day the power of these vast intentions will become as great as the aim of our wishes, prayers, and offerings.

Some practitioners who seem to have good intention may show the signs of inner faults when they meet with circumstances. For instance, someone may seem to have the intention to liberate all beings, but his main intention may actually be the wish for spiritual prestige that comes from the passion of pride. However, if he discovers this about himself, he may be able to transform it by the strong intention which uses the passions to turn us toward Dharma. Through the influence of Dharma, the passions can be seen as they truly are. By the blessings of the continuous presence of the wisdom teacher in our mind, the five passions can be transformed into the five wisdoms.

Some people who start to practice say that they do not feel anything and so they stop. This is because their main intention is to create pleasant feelings and happiness in this life rather than to attain enlightenment, which is unending, nonsubstantial exaltation beyond momentary feeling. Even though emotions change, and whatever changes is not valuable, if some people do not immediately feel better, they lose their faith. This happens because of the nihilist habit of believing in the importance of temporary feelings and not believing in nonsubstantial wisdom that comes through practice. They do not realize that the weakness of their practice is not from any fault of Dharma, but only the fault of their own intention, lack of faith, and the ripening of previous, negative karma that prevents them from practicing. Yet even if they stop practicing, they will not have an antidote for unpleasant emotions and their unfortunate karma will continue. Instead of withdrawing from practice, they must confront their obstacles in order to be released from them to attain enlightenment. Then, even if they wish to have positive emotions in this life, they can create them by continuing to practice, which causes positive phenomena. Emotions naturally become positive and the mind becomes stronger through the energy of intention and the commitment of faith. By not following after the first instant's negative emotion, but immediately trying to change it by thinking of Buddhas and watching, the second instant becomes positive and the first instant is gone. Mind is only deluded when it is dualistic. Sole awareness mind is emptiness and does not remain anywhere. By abiding in the recognition of nondualistic mind, negativity does not exist.

Dharma supports and encourages us even momentarily in this life, creating tranquillity. By practicing with faith, the mind is influenced by conceptions of sublime beings' qualities, which creates positive energy within the channels, airs, and essence of the body. In this way, Dharma helps us even if we only consider its temporary benefit according to nihilist measurements of positive physical and mental effects. Sometimes, when people are unhappy because of disastrous and tragic circumstances, no one can help them feel better. They can only comfort themselves by believing in deities and meditation. Then they can go to their altar and transform their circumstances through visualization and meditation, and their practice can bring them whatever they need. If they can abide in nondualistic mind, they cannot find their dualistic mind, so it is impossible to find any tragedy or dualistic emotion.

Although it is best to practice with emotions, if they do not arise, it is unwise to think that our practice is not sufficient. Whether emotions are dormant, apparent, unpleasant, or pleasant, they are only the expression of circumstances and are, therefore, unpredictable. If, because of dullness, there are temporarily no pleasant emotions, we may become upset and angry so that unpleasant emotions come through this circumstance. We can also create emotions intentionally if we wish to have emotions to support our practice. But without waiting for or depending on emotions, we must just practice and push ourselves to continue. Practice means that no matter what circumstances occur, we do not stop practicing until practice is naturally transformed into the state of nonpractice, which is enlightenment.

Emotions are wasted unless we can use them for practice. If we are practicing, our time and energy are never wasted because we are creating the seed of positive Buddha phenomena. With commitment, faith, and devotion, thinking of ourselves as inseparable from Buddha, we must watch our mind. Whenever emotions come strongly through circumstances, we must again think of Buddha and watch our mind. Since emotions do not exist anywhere but are only habit, they disappear by themselves. If we think about relative phenomena like emotions, relative phenomena will increase. In order to reach enlightenment, we are trying to forget whatever is relative. As long as we have habit, we do not do this by ignoring or denying relative phenomena, but through meditation, until there is only one sole, stainless mind in which no self or relative truth exists. When we have the phenomena of relative truth, we can pray and offer to Buddha. But when we either dissolve into Buddha or Buddha dissolves into us, Buddha is not different from us but inseparable with us.

Even negative emotions can be used for practice. There is no problem of negativity when emotions are transformed. According to the superior teachings of Mahāyāna, since wisdom is the pure essence of the passions, the passions are indications of the wisdoms which are present within one's own mind. Without the passions, wisdom cannot be introduced. If samsaric phenomena occur, it only means that the passions are apparent since they are being used and wisdom is dormant. That is when the wisdom within each sentient being is called Buddha nature. If wisdom is opened, whether through philosophical study or from sitting in one place in the samādhi of non-dualistic mind, and whether it is named with coarse or refined words, this opening comes from paying attention with awakened mind, which is the guide to the pith of the passions. When inexpressible awareness mind is realized through faith in the speech of sublime beings, inconceivable wisdom naturally blossoms without any effort of attention. As the omniscient Dharmabhadra said:

> The sky has no obvious appearance,
> But it pervades everywhere.

Sometimes the experiences of practice are given a lot of importance by new practitioners, who become attached to them. But actually, although experiences inspire us to have faith so that we can go beyond ordinary samsaric phenomena, having experiences means that there is still a connection with substance. All experiences only exist in relation to the practitioner's path of enlightenment and not in relation to the result of enlightenment, since they still exist within circumstances. As long as there is attachment, there is experience. All practice has the intention of increasing new experiences in order to release us from former experiences until we are released from all experience to the natural quality of enlightenment.

Each of us must find the basis of faith from within our own mind. Because the qualities of wisdom mind and the appearances of the Buddhas are unobstructed, there is no end to the reasons for having faith. The teachings of many Mahāyāna texts reveal that all sentient beings have Buddha nature and can be the same as the omniscient Buddha. For example, in the teaching of *The Uttara Tantra,* these three explanations are given. First, Buddha nature manifests from the minds of all sentient beings. This means we can have faith that all sentient beings have the potential of enlightened mind. Second, this self-nature is not different from the nature of any other Buddhas and does not have smaller or larger qualities, lower or higher qualities, or any qualities that can be distinguished from the Buddhas. This means we can have faith that within every sentient being, including ourselves, there is the full potential of complete Buddhahood. Third, all sentient beings are lineage holders of the essence of the Buddhas. This means we can have faith that this lineage has no possessor and is held by every sentient being through inherent Buddha nature, which must only be acknowledged as already true.

It may be asked that if sentient beings have Buddha nature from the beginning, then why are the immeasurable qualities of the Buddhas not apparent in them as they are in the Buddhas? They are not apparent only because sentient beings are not manifesting Buddha nature's self-display due to the obscuration of their lack of faith. The inconceivable qualities of the Buddhas are always apparent because there is no delusion and no division from the display of awareness. It is only because sentient beings twist these inherent, immeasurable qualities into obstructed substance that they are not obvious. As the Triumphant Victor in All Directions, Mipham Chhogle Namgyal, said, a sword has the power to cut, but this power is temporarily inconspicuous when the sword is sheathed. A stainless mirror has the limitless power to reflect, but this power is temporarily inconspicuous when the mirror is placed in a box. If the sword is removed from its sheath or if the mirror is removed from its box, the power of its qualities becomes apparent. When Buddha nature is recognized and used, sentient beings become the same as Buddha.

The awareness of Buddha nature that inspires faith automatically opens in practice. Even though the mind remains temporarily obscured through dualistic habit and intangible, stainless, totally transparent, unobstructed awareness is not known completely, there is still a connection between the meditation of the ordinary mind of practice and the pure awareness of great emptiness, like water which reflects the sky. Although the sky is formless and unobstructed, water reflects sky form, like the reflections of the mind which demonstrate and indicate great emptiness. So, just as the intangible sky can be reflected in water, wisdom mind can be reflected in the mind that is still obscured.

According to the inner Vajrayāna teachings, the five skandhas of form, feeling, perception, intention, and consciousness are the five Buddha families of Tathāgata body, lotus speech, vajra wisdom mind, jewel quality, and all-accomplishing activity. Whoever holds Vajrayāna samaya but does not realize this is breaking the eighth vow of the fourteen Vajrayāna samayas. This vow is that one cannot insult the five skandhas since they are actually the manifestation of the five Buddha families.

If we ask how the five Buddha families exist within the five skandhas, the answer is that sentient beings have only built the five skandhas by not recognizing the five Buddha families. Whoever attains realization cannot find anything other than the five Buddha families. The ordinary five skandhas do not exist. This may seem impossible because of the misconception that the five skandhas can be separate from the five Buddha families, since they can diminish, be destroyed, die, and be born. Actually, from the beginningless beginning, the five skandhas are the inseparable, indivisible, deathless, birthless five Buddha families, if we can only believe that any other conception is the momentary phenomena of habit which comes from not recognizing the deities of the indestructible five Buddha families.

When deity is attained, the five Buddhas are the same as one's own awareness mind, which is beyond substance and destructibility. When all appearances are transformed into this sole essence of one's mind, which is already natural deity, there is nothing left of dualistic skandhas, so who separates? Who diminishes? Who dies? Who is born?

There are countless names for the different qualities of deity, but these qualities can be synthesized into the three categories of the origin of deity, the nature of deity, and the manifestation of deity. The origin of deity is immeasurable, stainless space. No one can affect it, and so it is the unconditionally triumphant wisdom hero. It is triumphant because the ordinary five skandhas and the demon of dualistic habit are defeated by the annihilating weapon of the realization of wisdom deity.

Whatever appears from the origin of this stainless, triumphant wisdom hero is reflection, so whatever wrathful or peaceful unobstructed form, sound, or awareness arises must be triumphant. This is the nature of deity, which is completely pure, natural appearance.

The manifestations of deity such as Buddha Śakyamuni, Pad-

masambhava, Tārā, Vajrayogini, Saraswatī, Mandarava, Yeshe Tshogyal, and countless sublime beings emanate blessings with supreme
forms, sounds, and awareness within the phenomena of sentient beings in order to benefit them. Statues, holy objects, wisdom speech
in the form of oral teachings or texts, holy sanctuaries, and pure visions are also manifestations of deity which appear so that sentient
beings can purify obscurations and accumulate merit and wisdom.

Various emanations of deity can manifest within soothing elements to comfort beings, such as trees and shelters when they need
protection, or food when they are hungry. When beings need a support on which to dwell, deity can manifest within the earth element
as land. When beings need to drink, deity can manifest within the
water element to quench their thirst. When beings are cold, deity can
manifest within the fire element to keep them warm. When beings
are fading from heat, deity can manifest as gentle wind within the air
element to cool and rejuvenate them. When beings are in the tunnel
of depression, deity can manifest as space to free them.

Even though natural deity is indestructible and has inexhaustible
qualities, whoever does not believe and does not have faith in this
from the habit of delusion will always destroy himself by going from
saṃsāra to saṃsāra. But by believing in the inconceivable, inexhaustible, infallible qualities of wisdom deity, sacred Dharmakāya is
recognized.

Until we no longer have any samsaric phenomena, we can rely
on wisdom that comes from circumstances. This means that we depend on the circumstances of teachers, teachings, and our own mind
to increase wisdom qualities until we recognize and abide with confidence in self-illuminating wisdom. With determined faith in the in-
surpassable Great Perfection, we can recognize that undeluded mind
is awareness mind, undeluded consciousness is wisdom mind, and the
undeluded basis of all phenomena is the stainless inseparability of
space and appearance.

Even though wisdom mind is inexpressible, inconceivable, and
without characteristics, in order to create faith and understanding in

new practitioners, it can be described as sole awareness free from dualistic mind. In order to reach characteristicless wisdom mind, we have to change our previous habits to new habits through faith, practice, and meditation. To expand awareness of nondualistic wisdom mind, practitioners depend on many methods that use the support of all of the accumulations of virtue, such as prayers, recitation of mantra, visualization, and meditation, following their chosen sadhanas according to their explanations. When meditation is influenced by wisdom mind, even the residual, impure phenomena of the practitioner that arise from the ordinary habit of previous lives can cause pure phenomena, just as gross fuel causes the light of a fire. With practice, the fire of meditation exhausts the fuel of residual, impure phenomena so that gross habits vanish and wisdom pervades.

The practitioner's experience of wisdom that comes from circumstances is extraordinary and pure in comparison to ordinary worldly phenomena because it does not cause any heavy, samsaric, solid suffering. Gradually, through practice, even subtle, tangible conceptions diminish as a sign of the approach of stainless wisdom mind. Because these subtle conceptions naturally disappear through self-recognition, there is no chance for them to cause the sediment of habit. For example, it is impossible to paint in the sky because there is no place for the paints to settle, just as conceptions cannot settle in the wisdom of clear space. It is not necessary to depend on wisdom that comes from circumstances when wisdom mind opens, completely free of circumstance, because this wisdom is not different from the enlightened mind of the Buddhas.

If we want to receive the blessings of enlightened awareness, we only have to increase our faith and devotion. The blessings of Dharma never decrease and are always present to connect with us. When we practice in order to recognize this, we must realize that when blessings are received, they must be contained and not scattered. Discussing practice with one's teacher can untie the mind. However, without having wisdom confidence that is not affected by circumstances, when inexperienced practitioners talk casually about practice to other ordinary people, it only creates material conceptions about what is wrong and right. This can cause obstacles for receiving the blessings of practice, disturbing our energy by creating conflict and contradiction. Since the purpose of practice is to develop wisdom energy, we must contain this energy with a clear, simple, single mind. It is very difficult to sustain radiant, inner light without being secret about one's practice. In this way, without dispersing it, we can preserve and deepen wisdom energy as it arises.

When heavy, thick obscurations and lack of faith prevent us from seeing pure Buddha appearance, the only method is to rely on one's own wisdom teacher who introduces Buddha nature through teachings, initiations, or by directly pointing it out. Even though there is a sun, without a magnifying glass, it is impossible for kindling to catch on fire. Likewise, even though there is immeasurable wisdom energy embodied in the Buddhas and Bodhisattvas, without a teacher, it is impossible for one's own Buddha nature to open.

True love and faith come from wisdom teachers who show us the actual meaning of these words. One must especially have faith in one's own wisdom teachers who are showing the path of enlightenment. As Drigung Kyobpa Jigten Gonpo said:

> If the sun of your devotion does not shine
> To the lama's form, the snow mountain body of
>   the four kāyas,
> The flowing water of blessings will not fall.
> So therefore you must persist with earnest devotion.

Teachers may manifest different qualities with different students, depending on the mind of each student. The kind of teaching that is appropriate for each person must be considered in order to keep from wasting their potential. Wisdom teachers are, as Rigdzin Jigmed Lingpa said, "according to relative truth, suitable with everyone's traditions, and according to absolute truth, the opposite of anyone's traditions." Buddha said that the best teacher is one who can teach according to individual capacities, adapting to the karmic phenomena of each being. There is no contradiction in teaching different students with different methods, since any method can be used if it benefits. The essence of all teachings is the same, which, according to the Bodhisattva's path, is vast love inspiring deep faith that releases beings from suffering and leads to enlightenment. Just as a cake is sweet from whatever direction it is eaten, the instructions of a wisdom teacher reflect whatever skillful means will release us to enlightenment so that each person's capacity is fully used, from whatever point of view we are taught.

According to the Buddhist tradition, Dharma teachers are not thought of in an ordinary way and must never be abandoned and forgotten once they have taught us. Buddhist teachers do not guide us only in this life. They guide us until we attain the same confidence as our teacher. By our belief that our teacher abides with all Buddhas, he guides us to be released from all ordinary, miserable phenomena to the clear, stainless ecstasy of enlightenment.

Even if we are not practicing in an elaborate way with many deities, all deities are included within our wisdom teacher, who has only positive qualities. Whenever negative habits arise, we must instantly think of these positive qualities and recognize our ordinary conception as habit. In this way, we can transform all habit into deity, whose essence is our teacher, whose essence is all Buddhas. The qualities of deity are inexpressible because they are inconceivable, but we can think that deity means flawless, complete, immeasurable, beneficial qualities that appear within tangible and intangible forms, sounds, and awareness. We have to practice with this realization, according to our own sādhana and tradition, thinking of our teacher-deity and being sustained within our teacher's phenomena inseparably.

Some people create confusion for themselves by giving up former teachers and beginning with new teachers. But according to Buddhist tradition, as long as we have taken refuge in the Three Jewels and in a teacher, we never abandon them. We do not take the vow of refuge until we find a new teacher, like renting a house until we find another one, but until we attain the state of enlightenment.

Loyalty is a samaya vow. If we resist what we hear from a wisdom teacher, we should look within at our negative habit and immediately try to dispel it without leaving a seed which could cause the habit of resistance in the future.

Some people are interested in learning about Buddhist ideas, but not about Buddhist practices. Yet without practice, natural wisdom qualities do not blossom. If they do not develop wisdom qualities, these people may later regret their interest in Buddhism, thinking that it did not work for them. Instead of having faith and practicing, they give up. This occurs because, from the beginning, their intention is to learn substantial ideas to use only for the temporary purposes of this life. Whatever they learn easily fades and is dispersed because it is only learned through conceptualization and is disconnected from the vast quality of original awareness.

If we want to have faith, we must have the intention to make a strong effort. In Dharma, it is necessary to make a complete commitment and to give one's life. Since everything in ordinary existence is temporary, created from habit, and continuously changing, the more we try to do, the more it becomes essenceless. We must think deeply about this and about what is actually true and meaningful. Since the nature of mind is unobstructed, whatever we aim for occurs. By acknowledging this, and through the experiences that automatically come from strong commitment, we must practice with the resolution to know our own minds and to change ourselves and other beings toward enlightenment.

For many people, the biggest obstacle to having faith is their impure perception, through which anything can be misinterpreted. If our spiritual qualities are undeveloped, it prevents us from being able to recognize profound qualities in others. Then, even if we are able to meet sublime Buddhist teachers and teachings, we do not understand how precious they are. If we are involved in Dharma activities and associating with others who are interested in Dharma, but we are not tasting the truth of Dharma through practice, we will not understand the meaning of Dharma through our own experience. Then we will not see the priceless, inexpressible meaning of Dharma clearly. We will only hold on to our ordinary perceptions without being able to recognize the extraordinary spiritual qualities of others. If we judge sublime beings with our worldly habit and negative projections, it only increases our own obscurations. Whatever is beyond worldly phenomena cannot be understood by worldly reasoning.

Unfortunate beings who are strongly attached to their own impure perceptions do not release them even with the most positive circumstance of the blessings of pure teachers. They only see their own obscurations in others. Instead of using their samsaric phenomena to create new, positive phenomena through practice, they have more faith in their obscured ideas and in incorrect snap judgments than in Dharma and their teachers. Even when a sublime teacher shows the path of enlightenment, people may misuse this opportunity and relate to their teacher as the object of their own samsaric conceptions instead of perceiving him as the reflection of enlightenment's wisdom qualities with which they can unite.

The qualities of sublime beings can only be recognized by developing increased awareness. For those who begin to see these qualities through their practice, faith arises naturally through the evidence of their own experience and the recognition of the purity of self-revelation. With practice, the influence of chaotic, unclear, impure perception is purified by the influence of the calm, clear energy of natural mind.

Wisdom teachers can assume any aspect that will benefit, appearing to us in whatever way will open us to our inherent wisdom qualities. For example, sometimes wisdom teachers may appear to criticize and disagree with their students while revealing the wisdom of discernment, and sometimes wisdom teachers may appear to accept and agree with their students while revealing the wisdom of equanimity. We can never judge sublime teachers with dualistic mind, since their activity is beyond ordinary understanding.

Whatever a wisdom teacher says and does is indefinite and depends on how it is personally understood. It is through our own personal, positive phenomena that we increase the natural qualities of awareness mind. With the fortunate karma of being able to meet a spiritual teacher who can introduce and reflect the nature of mind, we can use whatever occurs within this precious connection to lead us to enlightenment.

The deepest meaning of teaching is not the form or aspect of any particular teaching, but the meeting of the teaching with the mind, in order to open wisdom mind. Actually, everything is teaching since everything is phenomena, and all phenomena are teaching if that is how they are used. Sublime beings can teach anything because wisdom mind is unobstructed and reflects everything through unconditional compassion. Buddha can be anything.

Actual teaching is to not know anything through dualistic mind, since the meaning of actual teaching is to reach enlightenment. By connecting to Buddhist teachings with faith, we can increase our own pure phenomena until they become the same as the empty, pure appearance of Buddha, who said, "I never said anything. Each sentient being just heard through their own phenomena." Since actual qualities come from within us, we must practice so that we can find inspiration from ourselves. The benefit of the compassion of Buddha comes from the phenomena of sentient beings. This compassion is completely natural and unobstructed without any condition of self or other, yet benefit occurs continuously and effortlessly as the result of previous aspiration and prayer.

If we want to develop continuous, vast love that is not affected by temporary circumstances, we have to create faith, since actual love comes from faith. Ordinary love that is not connected to faith depends on the changeable reactions of others, decreasing or increasing according to how it is rewarded and capable of turning into hatred or indifference. This kind of love has expectation and is not truly giving. Ordinary, nihilist love always eventually causes regret because it expects an ordinary, tangible reaction, going from one expression to another expression and from one substantial form to another substantial form. Even when others respond to our ordinary love for them in the way we wish, their response can never be ultimately fulfilling to us. Although others may want us to love them in a particular way, we may give them another form of love that is not what they want. Then, even though we give love to others with positive energy and kindness, it may create a negative reaction from them since it does not take the particular form they desired. Instead of increasing love, our love for others may cause frustration and an opposite reaction of unkindness, since all qualities in saṃsāra have the potential to turn into their opposite. Because there is never any lasting, matching connection in ordinary love due to previous karmic imbalances, it eventually causes dissatisfaction, unhappiness, and depression and leaves us caught between our hopes and disillusionments.

The compassionate, giving love of sublime beings is always without expectation, never causes regret, and always connects to us since it is unceasing. Through previous karmic obscurations, we may not recognize this actual continuous love. But without doubting, if we try with deep faith to increase the source of this love, which is the unconditioned awareness of our own wisdom mind, love arises naturally.

Sometimes practitioners with high realization who are filled with great love for others as a result of the strength of their practice seem to act outrageously and carelessly because they have no attachment to worldly phenomena or consideration of social customs. This is not the same as ordinary people who act outrageously. Although these ordinary people do not seem to care about what others think or expect, they are in fact very concerned with their own well-being and will feel unhappy when they have negative circumstances. In contrast, actual practitioners who have gone beyond ordinary phenomena become extremely careless about themselves, but care deeply about others. They are no longer seriously affected by circumstances since their own pure phenomena are so much more powerful from wisdom awareness. By this blessing, their activity benefits others naturally. The spontaneous activity of enlightened mind is completely beyond dualistic understanding but always manifests with the essence of this great compassion.

It is necessary for us to create an object of love through the great wisdom cynosure of sublime beings' presence. Then, we can make the wonder of spiritual qualities blossom through faith, including the incomparable love of compassion. By becoming the same as the Buddhas through their blessing, many beings will be drawn to our love-giving qualities, just as bees hover around the sweet-smelling scent of a lotus although the lotus itself has no idea or wish to attract bees. Even though growing from saṃsāra's mud, the lotus is unobscured and unaffected by it, opening its perfumed petals and giving its fragrance without expectation. When love is interwoven with faith, it is a manifestation of spiritual energy that benefits other sentient beings and is a natural offering to sublime beings. As it is said:

> There is no method to make Buddhas happy
> Other than to satisfy all beings.

As Rigdzin Jigmed Lingpa said in one of his prayers:

> Whatever brings benefit to sentient beings brings benefit to the
> Victorious Ones. So therefore, as Buddha said, 'I myself and
> all sentient beings share the same suffering and happiness.'
> Through this quality of the true nature of sublime beings, may
> you protect beings from suffering.

By hearing and believing in Buddha's speech and practicing with deep faith, pure and continuous love can increase until it is unaffected by any ordinary attachment. Through the wisdom of discernment which arises from faith, all phenomena can be understood distinctly, so that what is not actual love and what is actual love become clearly known. Whatever is known through the nongrasping wisdom of discernment never causes any negativity toward other beings or any self-hatred because it is inseparable from the emanation of great kindness. Through the qualities of the interdependence of phenomena that arise, the power of the energy of this love connects to others and can extend to many beings. Vajrayāna practitioners are especially able to develop love that is independent of external phenomena by transforming all beings and circumstances into immeasurable, loving deity phenomena through visualization and determined mind. Because of the influence of stainless wisdom, these practitioners have no expectation of obvious, ordinary, dualistic love from others since they are already complete with nondual, desireless love that does not grasp at self or others. When the limited love of previous nihilist habit expands into the great kindness of Bodhisattva's munificent love, it is unendingly compassionate even when extended to all beings, giving positive energy to them whether or not anything is received in return. This great love comes from the faith which connects us to the blessings of sublime beings' wisdom mind so that everything, including love and faith, becomes deep and pure. Then ultimately, without any expectation, conditions, or intention, love becomes the unobstructed emanation of the limitless, aimless, natural love of the great compassion of enlightenment.

The Seven-Branch Prayer of the Accumulation of Merit

Absolute, inherently born wisdom mind
Only comes from the handprint of the
    purification of obscurations and great
    accumulation
Or from being blessed by a highly realized
    guru.
You must know that to try to depend on
    another method than that is foolish.

— MAHĀSIDDHA SARAHAPA

Sole awareness light mind is self-accomplishing accumulation, according to Mahāsandhi. Nothing can cause ordinary substance because appearances do not separate from stainless Dharmakāya. Since there is no dualistic clinging or anyone who clings, everything is the array of wisdom's self-accumulation. But it is very rare to realize and abide in this state unless one has a gifted mind, so most people must practice, accumulating virtue and wisdom.

When we are in formless, sole space meditation, which is the state of abiding in nonduality, it is actual accumulation. At that time, we do not need to make accumulation with the appearances of phenomena. But whenever we move from this state and the appearances of habit occur according to the Hīnayāna and Mahāyāna teachings, or the display of unobstructed quality occurs according to the precious Vajrayāna teachings, we must try to transform all appearances into pure phenomena through accumulation.

135

In the Hīnayāna, Mahāyāna, and Vajrayāna traditions, there are countless methods for the accumulation of virtue. The seven-branch prayer is always included within each of these traditions and can be practiced according to the point of view of each particular sādhana for the accumulation of merit and wisdom. But because we believe more strongly in the reality of ordinary mind than in the intangible presence of Buddha nature, accumulation is neglected and misunderstood.

In this degenerate age, the great Buddhist teachings are often misinterpreted through nihilist habit. If Buddhist philosophy is studied, it is used to build self-assertive, intellectual philosopher's ego in order to acquire and support one's position in this present life rather than to subdue ordinary mind and realize wisdom mind. If yoga is practiced, it is used to make the karmic body healthier and more shapely for this momentary life rather than to develop wisdom energy through which deathless wisdom body is attained. If retreat is done, it is used to boast to others about the quantity of one's accomplishments in order to create a false siddha ego rather than to change the defiled energy of samsaric phenomena into the positive, pure phenomena of wisdom deity. If precious teachers are met, instead of respecting them and receiving their wisdom blessings through our devotion in order to awaken Buddha nature, there is only a wish to become their intimate friends in an ordinary way, to look important to others and gain status.

It is a disaster when beginning students of Buddhism who do not have weariness of saṃsāra or faith in enlightenment misuse the profound words belonging to vast points of view such as "freedom from mental activity" of Mādhyamika's teachings, "the pervasiveness of natural mind" of Mahāmudrā's teachings, and "liberation from the beginning" of Mahāsandhi's teachings. Their mouths say these words without clearly understanding their deep meaning, since their minds do not abide in these great states. Instead, as a result of previous, strong karmic habit, their minds are continuously engaged with delusion. They can only return to their involvement with ordinary phenomena and their old samsaric habits, without liberating themselves from these habits. As a sign of impending apostasy, they may talk with arrogant energy, step on sacred texts or Buddha's pictures, and dismantle their altars. As a result of their strong habit of disbelief, they do not try to accumulate virtue through their reverence for enlightenment. They only grab at Dharma's precious words in order to build ordinary ego. This actually prevents the attainment of enlightenment. Whatever prevents enlightenment through impeding the accumulation of merit is samsaric habit. If this misinterpretation is made, positive karma is not created because there is no belief in the accumulation of merit and wisdom and no belief in the Buddhas.

Buddhism's highest teachings which say that there is nothing that needs to be done are used by some people as an excuse for their laziness and lack of faith. They then neglect or disregard accumulation, while continuously collecting the refuse of saṃsāra. But just as the treasure of water increases in the rivers of summer, it is better to increase the accumulation of merit and wisdom, believing that mind is continuous, in order to attain the state of enlightenment.

In all the traditions of Buddhism, sublime beings are worshiped to attain enlightenment. If we think that this practice is just using our imagination, we are missing the point of view. Imagination is considered to be unreal thinking. But whatever we believe becomes true to us, so if we believe in something, it is not imaginary. Until sublime beings actually appear to us, it may seem that worshiping them is only imaginary. Yet we must realize that as long as we are deluded, everything is imaginary and created by mind.

Everyone uses imagination in an ordinary way, although this has no ultimate benefit. When we worship sublime beings, instead of just using ordinary imagination, we are using our mind's ability to create pure phenomena with visualization, prayer, and offering, which have the immeasurable benefit of connecting us with unceasing, inconceivable mind. Believing in and practicing with pure deity benefits us in this life and always because it causes the pure energy of positive phenomena to manifest until we attain the infallible wisdom of Buddha.

Sublime objects cannot be compared to any ordinary objects.

But sentient beings always create and cling to ordinary objects, which only lure, deceive, and give us suffering. Instead of trying to temporarily console ourselves with these heavy, samsaric objects, we can transform them through our practice into sublime, light deity phenomena, which bring ultimate comfort. This can happen just through believing and trying. As great, ancient scholars have said, when we practice to attain enlightenment continuously and with endurance, nothing else is difficult, just as when we are under water, the rain does not affect us.

Practicing with the myriad aspects of sublime beings is not for the purpose of finding temporarily comforting spectacles, but to awaken our ordinary mind into an awareness of sublime beings' appearances. Through believing, we can transform our ordinary karmic body into wisdom deity body, our ordinary reality into dustless wisdom pureland, and our ordinary worldly energy into the power of wisdom energy, which never harms and always benefits.

Because we cannot concentrate or practice without attachment, we must first increase attachment to the pure qualities of deity in order to encourage ourselves to practice. When we have experiences such as positive dreams or visions, we must release our attachment to them to keep from causing self-righteous demons. We must practice with a stainless space point of view until our attachment to deity transforms into the natural nonattachment of wisdom appearance.

If we have a gifted mind and fortunate karma, we can practice according to the inner tantric system without distinguishing between subject and object. We can visualize whatever deity we wish in a benevolently wrathful, peaceful, desireless, or desirable aspect, depending on our previous karmic connection to these deities. Through this practice, we can increase the phenomena of wisdom deity until we become the same as indivisible wisdom maṇḍala.

Although a farmer plans to grow fruit, he incidentally creates other results such as leaves and flowers. In the same way, although a practitioner intends to reach enlightenment, he incidentally creates other positive results such as the increase of sublime energy corresponding to the nature of the deity of his practice. Peaceful deities unintentionally manifest wisdom qualities which soothe gentle beings through predominantly pleasing, attracting energy in order to lead them to enlightenment. Wrathful deities unintentionally manifest wisdom qualities which conquer vicious beings through predominantly fearless, furious energy in order to lead them to enlightenment. Because the power of the senses is intensified by faith, the strength of one's intention is increased and whatever one wishes is accomplished easily.

In the same way that we would ask someone to bring us water if we were thirsty, we must pray to sublime beings to quench our thirst for wisdom with their elixir of enlightenment. Praying to request their help and support to be guided toward enlightenment diminishes the suffering which comes from meaningless, ordinary gossiping and purifies the obscurations of speech which come from impurities of many lives' karmic airs. Just as, when we sing a beautiful song across a mountain valley, its melody echoes back to us from the mountain, by praising, chanting, and praying to intangible sublime beings, we can hear the celestial song of wisdom through the power of having created self-flourishing, beautiful sounds ourselves. Prayer unites us with Buddhas' unobstructed, melodious wisdom speech and makes the auspicious connection to be able to teach other beings precious Dharma.

Like a child who cries out to his mother for protection when he is afraid, we must ask sublime beings to protect us from samsaric fear and guide us to the safety of enlightenment. Remembering the awful suffering of saṃsāra with fear and remembering the wonderful qualities of enlightenment with devotion, we take refuge with the wish for all beings to attain the state of enlightenment. Instead of being distracted by our dualistic mind's paranoid, negative projections, if we concentrate toward the pure, positive, most powerful phenomena of the Triple Gems, we will not have even one impure thought, so there will be no more cause of fear. Then our mind will become pure, profound, and egoless, and we can join with the sole, clear, fearless appearance of Buddha's wisdom mind.

When we practice, we are surrendering to enlightened beings.

This is not ordinary surrender, temporarily giving up our power to an ordinary object for some ordinary reason. It is giving up our ego's need for power and surrendering to sublime beings in order to transform our ego into egoless deity.

Ordinary surrender is temporarily giving up ordinary power in order to gain more ordinary power. However, when circumstances change, surrender based on an ordinary intention turns into resistance and defensiveness in order to protect our ego. Submitting to an ordinary authority is entirely different from surrendering to beings who have enlightened awareness, which increases egoless wisdom power that never diminishes through being open to receiving their blessing. If we surrender to an ordinary object, the result will always be limited. If we surrender to the Triple Gems, the result will never be limited.

Even if we do not like to surrender because of our ego's habit of freedom, surrender is unavoidable. Since there is always some aspect of inequality among beings, there is always the difference of lower and higher status, with dependence and surrender. No one can be really free because we all meaninglessly surrender to each other. As long as we are already surrendering, it is more beneficial both temporarily and ultimately to surrender to the greatest solace, which releases us from ordinary surrendering.

Unless we are sincerely devoted to practice, we cannot understand the profound meaning of surrender. We can fool ourselves endlessly about our practice unless we realize that ultimate confidence only comes from surrendering to sublime beings.

True surrender comes from deep, pure, continuous reverence. If we honor Buddha's inconceivable teachings with sincere and noble devotion, they show us through our own experience the reason to respect wisdom qualities. Respect for self-awareness wisdom is the recognition that Buddhas guide all sentient beings away from the suffering of delusion. When there is no delusion, there is no cause of samsaric suffering. The essence of nonsuffering is to be in awareness mind. We must simply believe and stay in that awareness. Surrender is the openness to clear, vast, limitless wisdom space. This openness means that we surrender through our practice to Buddha and his precious teaching, to luminous deity phenomena, to all visible and invisible sublime beings, including our teacher, and to our own wisdom mind.

One's own mind is intangible and unobstructed, so that anything is ready to appear through its creations, since all that appears is manifested by mind. In order to join our conception of intangible deities to actual, inconceivable deities, we must revere their qualities so that their presence can be reflected within our own phenomena, which is always meaningful.

Until we reach enlightenment, we must take refuge in the Buddha, Dharma, and Sangha with compassion for all sentient beings. Then, to practice the seven-branch prayer of the accumulation of merit, we must do prostrations thinking that all sentient beings are with us in order to dispel the pride of samsaric ego. We must offer our body, speech, and mind with immeasurable samādhi sky treasure appearances, including all positive samsaric phenomena and all pure, vast, miraculous Buddhafields, in order to dispel our greed and desire. We must confess the cause of all sentient beings wandering in saṃsāra throughout all lifetimes, which is the lack of faith in Buddhas' precious, most meaningful teachings, in order to dispel our anger and hatred. We must rejoice in the worldly virtues of ordinary beings and in the flawless virtues of sublime beings in order to dispel our jealousy. We must request all Buddhas to turn the wheel of Dharma for the benefit of all sentient beings in order to dispel our ignorance. We must beseech the emanations of all Buddhas to unceasingly remain within sentient beings' phenomena until saṃsāra becomes empty, in order to dispel our wrong views. We must dedicate any virtue, not just for a temporary goal or aspiration, but for all sentient beings, including ourselves, in order to dispel our doubt and reach enlightenment.

Prostrations mean the expression of humility and respect toward those who have sublime qualities, which purify the obscurations of our ordinary, arrogant egos. If we are not wild animals, we inevitably respect others anyway through worldly customs and gestures of humility, such as asking others to walk, sit, or eat before we do, even though this ordinary respect is ultimately useless. Through doing prostrations, we show our reverence for the sublime power of wisdom mind in order to reach enlightenment.

Prostrations help us to develop humility and serenity of the mind and relieve physical tension, untying the knots of the channels so that energy can flow smoothly. In the same way that a young dancer's body is reflected back to him from a stainless mirror, naturally cleansed of impurities through the movements of his dance, prostrations to the Three Jewels release blockages of karmic channels and airs and purify karmic obscurations, particularly the obscuration of pride, permeating us with wisdom blessings and bringing the joy of deities' celestial wisdom form, making the connection to join with Buddhas' indestructible, luminous wisdom body.

Offering means giving to honor those we believe are higher than us. For example, benevolent kings are offered gifts as a sign of gratitude and honored with respect as a sign of confidence from their thankful subjects. Offering to sublime beings is the expression of gratitude for their great kindness and of our wish to make the connection with them to receive their blessings.

If we are asked to make offerings to intangible sublime beings in order to increase inexhaustible, intangible, selfless qualities, we become reluctant and think it is foolish. We would rather entertain ourselves and our friends for momentary pleasure. If we are asked to offer one flower on an altar to Buddha, we think it is too costly and are afraid it is a waste. If we are asked to fill a vessel with water to offer to Buddha, we become lazy and think it will take too much time and energy. If gods and deities are imperceptible to us because of the habit of nihilism, we think there is no purpose in offering to them. Yet the idea of giving to worldly beings does not seem absurd at all to us, even though the intention and result are limited.

Without any doubt in our mind, offering inexhaustibly to powerful sublime beings for the accumulation of virtue with the vast intention of releasing all sentient beings into enlightenment is the profound method that is the cause of exhausting our dualistic, desiring mind, which can transform into selflessly generous Bodhisattva mind. Offering in this way purifies our feelings of poverty and the obscuration of greed, enabling us, until enlightenment, to be born in a noble land with wisdom phenomena so that we can join with the inexhaustibly abundant aspects and appearances of the Buddhafields' immeasurable wisdom qualities.

Confession means apology. At a worldly level, if we do not tell others we are sorry when we have done something wrong to them, we cause problems between ourselves and others and prevent ourselves from cultivating qualities of nobility. Just as we would apologize to a friend we have offended, if intentionally or unintentionally we have broken the vows or samaya we have taken according to the tradition we are following, confession to powerful, sublime beings purifies our obscurations in order to reach enlightenment.

Admitting our faults dispels our ignoble habit of deceit and denial and purifies the obscuration of anger, increasing our habit of honesty and purity so that our mind becomes tranquil and we can receive wisdom blessings, just as a white moon beam opens the moon lotus. Ultimately, we can go beyond conceptions of wrong and right, joining Buddhas' great, stainless, clear space equanimity.

Rejoicing means happiness for the good fortune and virtue of others, which is actually our joy in the intangible qualities of mind that are their source. Although we may think that it is absurd to rejoice in the virtues of others as a way to accumulate merit, we still appreciate others' ordinary positive qualities, even though we do not think it causes any ultimate benefit for anyone. Rejoicing as spiritual practice destroys the selfish, jealous qualities of our self-seeking ego and increases the positive intention to develop our mind's capacity to accept the positive qualities of others, which increases positive qualities in our own mind and purifies the obscuration of jealousy. We must especially rejoice in the spiritual qualities of others and in their practice. Even if one is not practicing oneself, by respecting the practice of others, and by encouraging and helping others to practice, one is rejoicing, so it is the same as practice.

Rejoicing in the virtue of others develops a vast, versatile mind which can adapt to anyone or to any circumstance, and which accommodates and accepts everything, like a bridge that always supports anyone who crosses over it. By creating the beauty of joy, we receive the sublime inspiration to join with Buddhas' incomparable, timeless, directionless wisdom activity.

Requesting Buddhas to turn the wheel of Dharma means asking them to teach us in order to turn us toward enlightenment. Even at an ordinary level, without requesting those who know more than we do to teach and help us, we cannot learn anything new, do what we want, or go where we wish. Just as we would ask for help to reach our destination if we were lost, we must request Buddhas to turn the wheel of Dharma to eradicate our ignorance through their immeasurable wisdom and guide us to sublime, destinationless enlightenment.

The request for Dharma teachings dispels our habit of unknowing and purifies our obscurations of ignorance, just as the radiant sun dispels all miserable darkness, bringing the clear light of wisdom knowledge that purifies all ignorance and causes sublime Dharma appearances. This creates the seed to become omniscient forever, like all-knowing Buddhas who effortlessly guide all beings to enlightenment through the profound expanse of their precious teachings.

Beseeching means begging the Buddhas to remain with us amid saṃsāra's suffering in order to help sentient beings, since we need them to show us how we can be released from suffering. Just as we do not want those we love to die but to be with us, we must beseech all Buddhas to remain with us for the benefit of guiding all sentient beings to enlightenment.

By beseeching all Buddhas to remain with us in saṃsāra, we can meet many sublime teachings and beings who are the emanations of Buddha, cleanse residual, negative karmic energy, and purify illnesses, obstacles to life, and the obscuration of disbelief. We will also be born with good karmic conditions and a long and healthy life. Just as a sunflower follows the sun in order to survive and produce an abundance of nourishing seeds, by opening to and following Buddhas' sun-faced teachings, we can always live long with our Dharma teachers because of the enlivening energy we create. The ultimate benefit of beseeching all Buddhas to remain with us in saṃsāra is to join with Buddhas' unborn, immortal, intangible, wisdom exaltation body.

Dedication means the resolution to have the ultimate aim. When we shoot an arrow, we need to have a target. In the same way, we must dedicate all accumulated merit to benefit ourselves and others, so that all sentient beings may reach the inexhaustible wisdom qualities of enlightenment. Ordinary dedication is the aim of creating virtue for the benefit of this present life, or for being born in the higher realms in future lives, in order to have the samsaric phenomena of happiness. This worldly dedication is ultimately false. The dedication of practitioners of the Bodhisattva path is to attain the state of enlightenment for the benefit of all sentient beings, to create happiness for others temporarily within samsaric phenomena, and ultimately to guide them to enlightenment.

After accumulating any virtue, it must be dedicated for all sentient beings. The reason for dedication is to prevent us from causing any substantial reality through dualistic, grasping intention and to enable us to abide in Dharmakāya forever, with intangible, immeasurable light Rūpakāya phenomena, which is the essence of all Buddhas.

Whenever virtue is accumulated, there is a threefold aim. For example, if one gives to pitiful beings, there is the object of the pitiful beings to whom one gives, the object of the material that is given, and the one who gives. If one is offering, there is the object of offering, which is sublime beings, the object of whatever is offered, and the one who offers. If one is praying, there is the object of the Triple Gems or one's own wisdom deity, who are the same, the object of the prayers with vast intention, and the one who prays. Whatever accumulation of virtue is made, whether it is according to the tradition of Hīnayāna, Mahāyāna, or Mantrayāna, it is very important to dedicate it with unfolding this threefold aim into aimlessness, in order to attain the stainless state of Dharmakāya.

The dedication of virtue increases virtue, purifies our mind's habit of vagueness and the obscurations of doubt, and results in the acquisition of many positive aspects of existence. If we pour drops of water onto the ground, they will soon dry and disappear, but they will never diminish if we pour them into the never-diminishing, ever-increasing ocean, since they are mixed inseparably. In the same way, when we dedicate whatever virtue we accumulate, it is never wasted. The ultimate benefit of dedicating all virtue for all sentient beings to reach enlightenment is to join with Buddhas' inexhaustible, omniscient wisdom ocean.

The Transitional States,
the Yogas, and the Kāyas

If you realize your own wisdom mind, that is all.
Nobody knows anything other than that.

— MAHĀSIDDHA SARAHAPA

Serious reaction to phenomena as reality is destructive because it causes energy to be disturbed, diminished, or lost. Practicing with the correct point of view causes the exhaustion of distraction toward phenomena as reality, enlivening the light form of emptiness so that positive tangible and intangible energy increases inexhaustibly and the qualities of the three kāyas can fully blossom.

In the Mahāyāna teachings, the three kāyas are described as the three permanences. Some followers of the Hīnayāna have thought this means an eternal permanence of phenomena that have a true, substantial existence, which would contradict the view of the Hīnayāna doctrine that all the compounded phenomena of reality are impermanent. But the permanence of the three kāyas in the Mahāyāna teachings does not mean the permanence of an unchangeable, self-existent god or of anything which exists only as an object perceived by a deluded ego subject. Instead, it means that the undeluded wisdom mind of all Buddhas continues permanently in one stainless, unchangeable essence of sky. The permanences of the pure phenomena of enlightenment of Nirmānakāya and Sambhogakāya are the qualities of measureless Buddhahood and are inseparable from the permanence of the great, indestructible emptiness of Dharmakāya.

147

According to the Mahāyāna view, nothing tangible or intangible can affect great emptiness, which is always unobscured and pure. This is called the essential permanence of Dharmakāya (chhoku ngo-wo'i tagpa). Dharmakāya is completely pure formless form.

The nature of Dharmakāya is unobstructed like stainless sky, so any wisdom qualities and aspects can manifest from its unobscured spontaneity. Since Dharmakāya is pure, whatever appearances radiate from it are self-adornments and always pure. This pure appearance is called the continuous permanence of Sambhogakāya (longku gyungyi tagpa). Sambhogakāya is immeasureable qualities of flawless, inconceivable, desireless exaltation form.

Infinite manifestations, whether they seem to be objective or subjective, can spontaneously and unendingly manifest from the pure appearance of Sambhogakāya to benefit beings. These reflections can manifest as many impure aspects to connect with the impure phenomena of sentient beings to guide them to pure phenomena, and as many pure aspects to connect with the pure tangible phenomena of sentient beings to guide them to pure intangible phenomena. Although the occurrence of these appearances is definite, their aspects are an indefinite emanation of effortless compassion to the indefinite faculties of countless sentient beings, arising in any form, at any time, and in any direction. This is called the indefinite permanence of Nirmānakāya (tulku ngepa medpa'i tagpa). Nirmānakāya is unobstructed, miraculous emanation form.

The quality of Dharmakāya is stainless, great emptiness. Since it does not have the permanence of an object, it never remains in the somethingness extreme of eternalism. Yet because of its unobstructed nature, pure wisdom appearances unendingly manifest so that it never remains in the nothingness extreme of nihilism.

Even ordinary karmic phenomena are obscured, impure manifestations of the three kāyas. For example, the state of deep sleep is the impure manifestation of Dharmakāya, beyond tangible and intangible, material appearances. Dreams are the impure manifestation of Sambhogakāya, arising as intangible, subtle appearances beyond daytime's tangible, gross appearances. Waking phenomena are the impure manifestation of Nirmānakāya, arising as tangible emanations of appearance. Through practice, these impure manifestations become the pure manifestations of the three kāyas as they naturally are.

The term "impure three kāyas" may be perplexing to some people if they have not heard an explanation of its meaning. It does not mean that there is ever any actual impurity of the three kāyas, since they are always pure. It means that they contain the infinite capacity to reflect anything, whether impure or pure. It is only through our lack of recognition of the three kāyas that their purity is temporarily obscured and dormant. Until enlightenment is attained, there are obscurations, and so there is impurity, but the purity of the three kāyas is still inherent. When the kāyas are called impure, it is only in order to demonstrate this purity. This subject is mentioned in many Mahāyāna texts, including *The Teachings of the Profound Inner Meaning* by Karmapa Rangjung Dorje, the Holder of Activity, Self-Occurring Indestructibility.

Just as the three impure kāyas have the potential to become the same as the three pure kāyas, all ordinary sentient beings have the inherent seed of Buddha nature and the potential to become the same as Buddha. The only difference between sentient beings and Buddhas is that sentient beings have not recognized their Buddha nature and are dwelling in ignorance, and Buddhas have recognized and are abiding in enlightenment. Because sentient beings are influenced by defiled passions, the elements become impure and manifest as impure phenomena that are perceived with impure senses.

By acknowledging Buddha nature, we are motivated to practice to transform our impure elements into pure elements. But if we have the nihilist habit of not believing in Buddha nature because of previous karma, it prevents us from devoting ourselves to practice. Because of this obstacle, we may not become enlightened immediately, although the potential of instantaneous enlightenment is always present. The teachings of the Buddhas reveal the method for opening this potential through practice to attain the wisdom of great exaltation.

This awakens ordinary mind to the Buddhas' mind of enlightenment, which is the transformation of the three impure kāyas into the three pure kāyas.

According to the general Buddhist point of view, dualistic mind exists continuously until enlightenment. However, dualistic mind does not function in the five states of unconsciousness, which are deep sleep, entering the equality of union, intoxication, the dullness of neutralized extremes, and fainting. Whatever names these states of unconsciousness are given, no matter how they are caused, and whether they last for only a moment or for many lives, they have the same essence of unawareness.

We may think that we are aware when we are engaged with phenomena, or that we are in a special state of mind when our awareness of phenomena is suspended. But as long as we remain in dualistic mind, both of these states are momentary and result from the delusion of the passions and the senses. They do not have any basis of actual awareness. Even our activity is only a form of indifferent stupor when its essence is unfocused and dull, and is as useless as the rippling water of a desert mirage. As long as we are not awakened in a state of stainless, primordial purity, we are limited to our ordinary, dualistic mind, which is always the cause of indifferent stupor.

From the Buddhist point of view, indifferent stupor is the unawareness of mind's clarity. When there is no clarity, there is no discernment, and so the countless, distinct qualities of phenomena are indistinguishable. Just as nothing can be seen in a dark room without light, our awareness is dimmed and blurred without clarity and discernment.

Indifferent stupor is the basis of habit and the cause of all the ignorance of saṃsāra. As long as we remain in this state, we do not have mindfulness about what we see, what we say, or what we think. We do not see the relation between an intention and its result. We cannot distinguish the difference between what is harmful and what is beneficial, or between what should be abandoned and what should be accepted. We continuously accept abandonable objects and circumstances, and continuously abandon acceptable objects and circumstances.

We foolishly feel comfortable in a state of dullness because of the thick, nihilist habit of countless lives. We may think that neither suffering nor happiness occurs within dullness, but if we examine this state carefully, we will see that it is actually the cause of suffering because it is the basis of ignorance and of saṃsāra. We must be released from this state through the grace of Buddha's precious teachings, which always have the power to awaken and lead us from the dangerous darkness of indifferent stupor to stainless, clear space.

Many people think that a transitional state (bardo) is a single state between this life and the next. Actually, the meaning of transitional states is any phenomena that exist other than primordial, stainless awareness. If phenomena are influenced by wisdom mind, they become the phenomena of the pure transitional state of the uncontrived, essential nature, which is dharmatā. Dharmatā means that whatever purity potentially exists appears naturally. Although this is pure, spiritual phenomena, these phenomena change. Therefore, because they change and do not constantly abide, they still belong to the transitional states. Whatever phenomena belong to dualistic mind, including the habits of the six realms of sentient beings, are the impure delusion of the transitional states through which sentient beings continuously circle as long as they remain in saṃsāra.

In the Vajrayāna tradition, which teaches how human beings can carry the transitional states to the path of enlightenment, there are systems of either four or six categories of transitional states. Many of the hidden treasure teachings of the Nyingma tradition reveal a system of six categories of transitional states, which includes the transitional state of life between birth and death (rangzhin bardo), the transitional state of dying (chhikha bardo), the transitional state of the uncontrived essential nature which is dharmatā (chhonyid bardo), the transitional state of the junction between past and future existences (sidpa bardo), the transitional state of dreams (milam bardo), and the transitional state of meditation (samten bardo). In the precious Nyingma Mantrayāna root text *The Inexpressible Expanse of Sound*, a system of four categories of transitional states is revealed, in which the transitional states of dreams and meditation are included within the transitional state of life between birth and death. Descriptions of all these categories can be found in many commentaries, so they are just briefly and simply explained here as a basis for introducing the way to be released from all transitional states through practice.

The unconditioned, natural state of Buddhas and its immeasurable phenomena are always equally pure. Therefore, all Buddhas are never in transitional states because they are always abiding in indivisible, vajra wisdom Buddhafields. Sentient beings have the same unconditioned purity as Buddhas, but through not recognizing the even purity of the reflections of mirrorlike mind, they moved into the uneven, samsaric phenomena of the transitional states.

The habits of previous passions which are the seeds of new habits come from the basis of mind (ālaya), and create all the six realms in which beings exist in the transitional state of life between birth and death. Whoever obtains a precious, human birth within this transitional state has the opportunity to purify all phenomena of the transitional states through studying and practicing. Then mind, which is obscured by the passions and by engagement with karma, can be purified and enlightened.

There are many different sādhanas and their commentaries that show how to be released from transitional states, following different traditions suited to different individuals' faculties and wishes. After we have chosen and understood our personal practice by listening to the instructions of our teacher, we can use our knowledge of the conditions of the transitional states by applying the basic ideas of practices that correspond to these states, such as those which are synthesized in the six yogas. This benefits any practice naturally.

The most important practices on the path of inner Vajrayāna are those of the visualization stage and the completion stage. Within the completion stage, there are practices both with and without characteristics that can be accomplished. For those who practice the Great Perfection, which is insubstantial and without characteristics (tshenmed), it is not necessary to also practice the completion stage with characteristics (tshenchay), as in the six yogas. But if practitioners wish, of course they may use these methods according to their faculties, using them as steps on the path.

The transitional state of birth and death is life in any of the six realms of rebirth, including the human realm, in which sentient beings exist as a result of their individual karmic phenomena. It begins at birth and continues until the circumstances of death. It is called a transitional state because mind has moved from primordial purity and is wandering in the suffering of the delusion of the habit of reality, unless the potential to return to primordial purity is recognized and attained through practice. Its duration depends on each individual's previously created karmic habit.

According to Buddhist tradition, the opportunity for release from the cycle of rebirth in saṃsāra exists mainly in the human realm, where it is possible to practice Dharma to reach enlightenment. In other realms, most sentient beings cannot be released from cyclic existence because the nature of life in these realms is not conducive to practice. Even within the human realm, there are negative circumstances which prevent people from benefitting from the freedoms and opportunities of a fortunate human birth.

To keep from wasting this human birth, all the activity of human existence should be connected to Dharma. Some people have a positive karmic connection to Buddhist teachings as a result of previous accumulations of merit, and automatically use whatever they learn for the ultimate benefit of all beings attaining enlightenment. It is this benefit that is the true purpose of traditional Buddhist subjects of study such as art, poetry, dance, medicine, biology, physics, astrology, semantics, linguistics, logic, philosophy, or the inner meaning of the quality of awareness. Other people may become knowledgeable but only use what they learn for their own temporary benefit in their present life. This is a misuse of knowledge that creates obstacles to breaking the ego since it does not have the ultimate, positive intention of reaching enlightenment for the benefit of oneself and others. Since it is not transparent and penetrating, knowledge obscured by ego blocks the view of openness and causes a limitation of awareness through weaving the curtain of cognitive obscurations.

If we are more interested in acquiring knowledge than in connecting knowledge to practice, there will not be any benefit even if we become familiar with many spiritual ideas. By holding one-sided views, engaging in unnecessary debate that distorts Buddha's teachings, and being fascinated with intellectual ideas that are not connected with wisdom, we can add pride to ordinary ego through equating knowledge with prestige. This only causes us to compare ourselves to others and results in the hope of being better than them, the fear of not being better than them, jealousy, and condescension, all of which are great hindrances to reaching enlightenment.

If we misuse knowledge to increase a bumptious sense of self-importance for our ego's worldly reputation, we cannot develop enduring, positive qualities which make us suitable vessels for Dharma, receptive to the precious qualities of sublime teachers and their teachings. We cannot learn anything new when we have decided that we already know everything. If we have a self-righteous ego, we limit our capacity to receive the blessings of Dharma, just as no matter how much nectar rain falls on a proud rock mountain, nothing is absorbed.

The essence of learning is being alert to our habits in order to change them. Then we can understand whatever we learn and we can be released from contradiction. Studying without the deeper learning of practice can cause misunderstanding through the development of the habit of intellectualizing. What seems to be logical thinking can create, rather than dispel, contradictions about Buddhist teachings if it is not based on a vast, authentically spiritual perspective. In order to be understood, Buddhist teachings may require the interpretation of sublime beings. If we only rely on an ordinary, intellectual understanding of spiritual ideas, without trying to practice, we will become extremely frustrated when our point of view cannot accommodate new knowledge or experiences that are beyond intellectual reasoning.

The experiences of practice cannot be expressed to nonpractitioners in ordinary words, but we may be more interested in expressing our ideas than in practicing. Although we may become intellectually exhilarated from hearing new information about Dharma, if what we hear does not register in our hearts, it will only make us more obstructed and superficial instead of more pure and deep. If we do not have the experience of practice, it does not matter how much we hear or express, since it will be essenceless.

It can only benefit us temporarily to collect ordinary, intellectual ideas about Dharma. If our ideas are based on a limited point of view and disconnected from Buddha's wisdom teachings, they may ultimately cause our negative qualities to increase. As Patrul Rinpoche said, this is "relying on Dharma, and then making the bad karma of non-Dharma." To prevent this from happening, when we enter the path of enlightenment, we should read and listen to the wonderful, awesome hagiographies of saints and Bodhisattvas who inspire us to make the commitment to subdue ego and increase boundless wisdom spiritual qualities.

Many people say that one must study in order to be knowledgeable, but it is rarely said that in order to be knowledgeable, one must practice. It is revealed in the sutras:

> Whoever knows Dharma, yet does not practice, is like a deaf musician who can make others happy, but cannot hear his own music.
> Whoever knows Dharma, yet does not practice, is like an expert navigator who guides others across the ocean, but dies at sea.
> Whoever knows Dharma, yet does not practice, is like those who can hear and see water, but cannot drink to quench their thirst.

And, as Kunkhyen Longchen Rabjam said:

> Since knowledge is like countless stars in the sky,
> The study of ideas is never exhausted.
> So in this life, it is better to realize the profound nature,
> The essential meaning of Dharmakāya.

Many sublime teachers have taught that in the transitional state of birth and death, we must enter the path of enlightenment without doubt, as an intelligent hawk enters her nest. Before building her nest, the hawk carefully chooses a safe location so that when it is built, she can approach it without hesitation. In the same way, we must first choose the teaching which corresponds to our individual capacity so that it can bring us to enlightenment through the gift of our connection to it. By hearing, studying, and contemplating the teachings with a determined mind, synthesizing them with unbreakable devotion to a sublime teacher, continuously practicing with the correct point of view, completely dedicating oneself to the path of enlightenment, and without having any doubt, confidence comes.

If we use the good fortune of our precious human birth for practice to reach enlightenment within the transitional state of birth and death, it can benefit us in all of the other transitional states. It is sometimes said that it is dangerous to do Vajrayāna practice, but there is nothing more dangerous than remaining continuously in saṃsāra. Everything is dangerous if we do not know what is ultimately wrong or right and we only guess with the limited judgment of ordinary mind, creating conceptions and circumstances with an indefinite result. It does not make sense to abstain from practice or turn away from Dharma out of caution or fear. The result of doing this for many lives is only to wander in the uncertain perils of saṃsāra.

The suffering of countless lives can only be uprooted within one life through the Vajrayāna method, by those who have devotion and the right point of view. It is not only in the many different methods of Vajrayāna practice that there are dangers, since any kind of spiritual ideas and Dharma that are misused with a wrong point of view can be dangerous. Instead of causing hestitation and doubt, we must study, learn, and especially practice this most precious Dharma until we have incisive confidence which is beyond all danger.

It is necessary for any practice to be done with the guidance of wise teachers until confidence is attained. There are many differences in sādhanas and their commentaries, and in individual capacities and experience. These must be assessed by one's personal teacher, and his instructions must be followed. Practices are not described here in greater detail in order to avoid confusion that could be caused by grasping at materialistic misinterpretations of more specific instructions and many different theories, but the basic ideas of practice are described in order to make a connection with the path of enlightenment.

These days, many students increase the possibility of misunderstandings by not recognizing the importance of receiving the blessings of lineage through depending on the instructions and experience of teachers. Instead, they try to take whatever they want to know from a book. As a result of their habit of believing in social equality, they perceive respect as tyranny and have a fear of honoring teachers. Inner Vajrayāna teachings especially, such as the six yogas, have to be practiced not only from reading books, but with faith and with qualified teachers, to prevent difficulties or disturbed energy which may result from the misunderstanding and misuse of these teachings. In these modern, degenerate times, people are interested in new worldly phenomena and new ideas in order to use them to create ordinary substantial conceptions, although they do not notice they are doing this. Even nonsubstantial Dharma teachings are misused in this way.

Ultimate knowledge of spiritual, wisdom qualities only comes through establishing the right point of view with one's own personal, intangible, stainless wisdom qualities and then practicing with any of the methods to attain enlightenment. This does not create substance. Since substance always depends on circumstance and whatever depends on circumstance belongs to saṃsāra, substance is always impermanent, diminishing, and exhaustible. Impenetrable, inextinguishable enlightenment is beyond ordinary beings' samsaric phenomena. Wisdom awareness and intangible qualities do not depend on circumstance and are free of all interconnected, samsaric phenomena. Within practice, substantial phenomena are only used momentarily, not to re-create ordinary phenomena, but in order to reach substanceless wisdom body, speech, and mind.

The practices of the tradition of inner Vajrayāna can be synthesized into the six yogas. All six yogas can be practiced within the transitional state of birth and death in order to be released from all transitional states. The explanation of the six transitional states and the explanation of the six yogas are automatically interrelated. Both only describe different aspects of one mind, which is the basis of the phenomena of the transitional states and the phenomena of practice, in order to increase the manifestation of positive appearance.

The Yoga of Magic Form,
Which Is the Basis of the Path

If we think that all appearances of impure and pure phenomena truly exist, then we are never released from saṃsāra's suffering, because we are trapped by the belief in reality. The practice of pure magic form is the transformation of all inner appearance into pure magic deity phenomena and all outer appearance into pureland magic phenomena, which is the samaya of the vessel initiation.

The essence of ordinary magic is deception; what does not exist seems to exist. Just as we are fooled by ordinary magic into seeing what is not there, if we believe in the tricks of ordinary mind's reality or unreality, we are only being lured. Actually, reality should be perceived as we would perceive the eight examples of magic: a mirage, a dream, an echo, a city of gandharvas, an illusion, lightning, a bubble, and magic.

We create endless samsaric phenomena and believe that they are real, even though they are only like a reflection of the moon in water. Although all outer phenomena are only our projection, we think that what we see is different from us. We continuously suffer because we try to keep what cannot be possessed.

Through the deluded magic of the extreme habit of believing in reality, we make a magician's illusions seem unreal, while making ordinary reality seem real, even though it is equally unreal. We think saṃsāra is true even though it is momentary, essenceless, and no more than impure black magic. To release all sentient beings from their black magic agony and from repeatedly being lost and losing, Buddha has revealed the pure magic phenomena practice of the inner tantric teachings. Pure magic is seeing all appearance as deity and pureland whose essence is always stainless emptiness, which never causes the suffering of samsaric reality.

To practice transforming the impure phenomena of reality into pure magic, the practitioner watches his image in a mirror. He imagines that this image is actually experiencing whatever he considers repulsive, such as being beaten, insulted with many abusive words, and tormented by others. When this suffering begins to seem real and a feeling of misery arises, the practitioner watches this feeling and asks himself, "Where is the pain? Where is the object that harms and the subject being harmed?"

Then, while watching this image in a mirror, the practitioner imagines that the image is actually experiencing whatever he considers desirable, such as being beautifully adorned, praised with admiring words, and cherished by others. When this pleasure begins to seem real and a feeling of elation arises, the practitioner again watches this feeling and asks himself, "Where is the pleasure? Where is the object that pleases and the subject being pleased?"

When we look in a mirror, we think our image is a reflection and our body is real. Actually, our "real" body does not exist anywhere and is just a temporary conception of form that comes from our previous habit of grasping. By this practice's manipulation of the distinctions between what is real and unreal, the practitioner can begin to understand that all divisions of real and unreal are relative. The mirror's reflection is empty form's empty body, which the most unpleasant phenomena cannot harm and the most pleasant phenomena cannot benefit. All insult and praise are like an echo.

After practicing this method of the mirror's magic empty form, the development of seeing unreality can be continued wherever conditions exist which increase the passions. While engaging himself with unfriendly and friendly people, experiencing negative and positive circumstances, the practitioner watches with the mirror of his mindfulness. These practices are done to lose the rigid, ordinary habit of reality so that mind can become nondual and transparent, opening to the nonattached display of the pure, magic, empty, clear appearance of deity.

When the mind becomes open, the practice of pure magic begins with the emanation form of deity. A new practitioner may use the method of observing the reflection in a mirror of a painting or statue of the particular deity, who is the essence of all deities, with whom he is karmically connected. Believing that he is the same as this deity, with no conception of the image as ordinary, tangible substance, the practitioner uses this method for concentrating and settling the mind until it becomes calm and steadfast. After this is accomplished, the wisdom deity's qualities are kept in mind while visualizing this deity in many sizes, from as small as a particle to as massive as a mountain. Countless deities are visualized as emanating from one deity, and countless deities are gathered into one deity. Sometimes the deity dissolves into space and the practitioner meditates. Again, the deity is visualized, appearing either gradually or instantly and miraculously. The visualization of wisdom forms, whether outer palaces and purelands or inner deities, should be undistorted and clear. Remembering and understanding the deity's pure qualities with the determination of the firm, unchanging, egoless pride of wisdom deity, the practitioner must completely decide that he himself is deity.

Since it is like magic, we may wonder how deity visualization can benefit us. But even without using visualization, our ordinary phenomena are like magic, meaningless and always changing. When we have positive, samsaric phenomena, we want to keep them, but since they inevitably change, we lose them and they cause us pain. The magic phenomena of Buddhas never harm us, fade, or change, because they are untouched by deluded mind's habit of samsaric phenomena. They are always luminous and like stainless sky, removing us from the habit of our perceptions of ordinary reality. Through pure magic, we can use our mind's mirrorlike quality, which can reflect anything unobstructedly.

The benefit of these practices is that one's karmic phenomena become less susceptible to samsaric influence through the truthless truth of the magic power of deity. The practitioner's deity phenomena can gradually flourish by cutting the old karmic habit of reality so fresh deity energy can appear, just as cutting the fading stems and leaves of flowers gives them refreshed energy to blossom.

The Yoga of Inner Heat,
Which Is the Root of the Path

The inner heat practice is the samaya of the path of secret initiation and purifies karmic phenomena through the ecstasy of unborn wisdom.

The essence of the main inner heat practice is to purify the air of karmic defilement through the development of wisdom air. But if this practice is only done with the ordinary air of ordinary mind and a worldly supernatural magic body, without establishing the vast wisdom point of view of enlightenment and without developing wisdom air, it still belongs to habit. Even though practice done in this way can produce temporary physical benefit and a worldly level of supernatural power may be accomplished, it only causes ordinary, miraculous change and does not belong to the stainless, enlightened, magic manifestations of Buddhas. A worldly-supernatural magic body may seem more powerful than a common karmic body, but they are actually both just impermanent, karmic results due to a previous emphasis on particular karmic phenomena. Instead of cultivating ordinary accomplishments within saṃsāra, it is most important to establish insubstantial, inconceivable, luminous wisdom air which manifests always as immeasurable, light wisdom Buddhafields.

At the beginning of this practice, all samsaric poisons of the karmic airs from the passions of many lives must be exhaled either three or nine times. Using the elements of the precious human body, the practitioner sits in the posture of Vairocana with the legs crossed in the indestructible position, the hands held in the gesture of equanimity, the back held straight, the shoulders spread open, the chin inclined slightly toward the neck, the tip of the tongue touching the upper palate, and the eyes gazing downward past the end of the nose. A simple, relaxed, cross-legged position can also be used.

The practitioner visualizes himself as the deity with whom he has a special karmic connection, with three inner channels and with the number of cakras indicated in the method of his particular sādhana. Then, the essence of wisdom air, in the aspect of the five pure elements, is visualized like a clean, clear rainbow, and is increased and retained as long as possible within the vessel of the body. The four methods of using air are practiced. These are drawing in wisdom air, filling the vessel of the body with wisdom air, refining karmic air with wisdom air, and expelling residual karmic air. During practice, karmic air is purified by being exhaled through the two side channels, and wisdom air is inhaled and retained in the central channel. The size of the central channel varies according to the methods of different practices done at different times. Wisdom air has no limitation of substantial form, but because practitioners have karmic air and the habit of form, the central channel is generally visualized as the size of the shaft of an arrow.

Below the navel in the central channel, the essence of wisdom bliss, the red nectar of great emptiness, is visualized in the aspect of a red syllable *ahshay,* like a thorn-shaped flame of heat that ascends through the central channel. At the top of the central channel in the head cakra, the essence of pure phenomena, the white nectar of skillful means, is visualized in the aspect of an inverted white syllable *hang.* As the heat of the flame increases, its color gradually changes from blue to red and ascends the central channel. Nectar drips from the white syllable through the heat of the flame, increasing greatest wisdom emptiness and bliss. Sustaining this experience brings the four rejoicings and the four emptinesses, which are inseparable. The four rejoicings are rejoicing, great rejoicing, supreme rejoicing, and simultaneously born rejoicing. The four emptinesses are emptiness, greater emptiness, greatest emptiness, and complete emptiness. Through these experiences, inherently born wisdom can be recognized by meditating in the uncontrived, essential nature.

This main practice is followed by branch practices using the sublime postures and movements of deity in the wrathful or peaceful aspect indicated in the particular sādhana that is practiced. Through the movements of miraculous mudrās, the karmic knots of the channels are untied and all karmic obscurations are purified. The wisdom channels are opened so that birthless, deathless wisdom exaltation can be attained. For the practice of inner heat, samaya must be kept until confidence is complete, holding vessel air continuously, practicing especially in cold places without wearing warm clothing or going to places with warm climates, and refraining from eating foods which cause obscurations.

Those who wish can practice further with either the inner, secret wisdom consort of the mind before confidence is attained, or with an outer manifestation of a wisdom consort. It is said in *The Sole, Wrathful Hero of Tantra*:

> For whoever has separated from desire,
> There is no more sin.
> There is nothing more fortunate than having bliss,
> So therefore, leaving your mind in equanimity,
> You must create the bliss of desire.

Those who have keen faculties and the capacity to practice like this must follow special teachings thoroughly and in a pure way, which is not for ordinary, licentious pleasure. This is the practice of the path of skillful means, which is the samaya of the wisdom initiation, in-

creasing substanceless great wisdom ecstasy to reach the union of the
state of Vajradhāra. But as Kunkhyen Longchen Rabjam said:

> Even though one thinks that one can progress on the path
>   through relying on another's body,
> By receiving the descending tigle of the third initiation,
> Many yogis deceive themselves with false practice.
> So therefore, sustaining the path of liberation is my heart's
>   speech.

The Yoga of Luminosity, Which Is the Essence of the Path

All form and formless practice is contained within stainless,
natural, luminosity space, which is the intangible source of enlightenment.

The main practice of luminosity is to try to recognize naturally
luminous emptiness. This practice can be done at all times, but especially just before sleeping at night and during light sleep at dawn. If
we do not practice with luminosity when we sleep, we immediately
lose consciousness and fall into the indifferent stupor of the basis of
mind without awareness. Then the samsaric dreams of our karmic
habits arise. Instead of letting this happen, it is very important for
inexperienced practitioners to pray to their root teacher-deity in order
to recognize luminosity. Rather than sleeping in one long period from
night to morning, it is better to try to sleep in short intervals, concentrating toward inseparable luminosity and emptiness while falling
asleep and awakening.

In a simple way, it is said in precious teachings that if one wants
to recognize luminosity, one should visualize one's root guru, inseparable with one's own awareness mind, in the center of one's heart in
the form of a stainless white sphere with a letter *ah*. One focuses on
this without any interfering thoughts while falling asleep.

The practitioner can also visualize himself as the deity of his sādhana, with the central channel in the center of the body as straight

and transparent as a crystal. In the heart center within this channel, the completely intangible syllable of the deity is visualized without grasping or tension, with clear light radiating everywhere. Wisdom air is retained to create a one-pointed focus. Then, with a relaxed mind, dissolving the visualization into luminous space, the practitioner meditates. Also, without dissolving the visualization, the practitioner can focus on the clear light syllable in the central channel of the deity of his sādhana, beaming throughout the vessel of the body like a lamp. If neither sleeping nor dreaming occurs and one has the experience of clear sky, it is the beginning of the recognition of symbolic luminosity. Gradually, when one gains experience in these practices, one can attain the confidence to stay in luminosity.

At the beginning of sleep, gross conceptions start to dissolve into emptiness. As sleep deepens, subtle conceptions begin to dissolve into greater emptiness. When sleep becomes still deeper, the karmic airs of conception dissolve into greatest emptiness. Then all gross and subtle conceptions end and all airs of consciousness are gathered into the central channel. Everything dissolves into complete emptiness with the final dissolution into stainless luminosity.

Although there are categories of the luminosity of the basis, path, and result, their essence is always the clear light of the mind. The luminosity of the basis is obscured through the mind's habits of the three realms of existence; the realm of desire, with tangible and gross conceptions, senses, and consciousness; the realm of form, with less tangible and more subtle conceptions, senses, and consciousness; and the formless realm, with only the intangible basis of subtle mind. Despite our lack of recognition, natural luminosity exists inherently within mind, even when these gross, subtler, and most subtle obscurations of mind conceal it.

The luminosity of the path can be recognized through previous good karma and the blessing of the guidance of a wisdom teacher who can reveal natural luminosity by purifying the obscurations of samsaric consciousness. All conceptions are purified through practice into sole, conceptionless, empty luminosity. The luminosity of the path includes the luminosity of dream practice, the luminosity of the time of death during the subtle dissolution of the elements, and the luminosity of meditation, which all originate in mind's natural luminosity. By continuous practice, one attains the luminosity of the result, the indivisible, boundless, indestructible unity of clear light.

Practitioners of the path of skillful means can increase the four emptinesses through the experience of the four rejoicings, using bliss and emptiness as the path for recognizing the final, complete, luminous emptiness.

Through luminosity practice, karmic airs and karmic obscurations are purified. At death, through actual knowledge of each of the stages of emptiness, we can recognize the stages of dissolving of the gross and subtle elements into the luminous emptiness of Dharmakāya.

The Yoga of Dreams, Which Indicates Confidence in the Path

Dream habit is caused by the recurrence of waking phenomena during sleep due to the force of karmic air and habit. In general, it is difficult to recognize that one is dreaming if, because of the habit of believing in reality, one cannot see while dreaming that the dream is unreal. Other interferences with recognition include being obscured by heavy energy, having many doubts about practice, eating irregularly and excessively, and being distracted by thick habits. So, in order to recognize that one is dreaming, these faults must be corrected with their opposites as antidotes. If the practitioner can transform ordinary dream phenomena into extraordinary deity phenomena and attain confidence in dream practice, it is proof that he can be liberated from the phenomena of samsaric reality in this life, in the transitional state of the juncture between past and future existences, or in the other transitional states.

A simple method is for the practitioner to visualize his root teacher in his speech cakra and pray to him to recognize his dreams as dreams. It is also said in precious teachings that to know he is dreaming, the practitioner can visualize his root teacher, inseparable with his own awareness mind, in the form of a stainless, white sphere with a letter *ah* in the center of the space between his eyebrows. He focuses on this while falling asleep in order to catch his dreams. Then, once he has recognized that he is dreaming, the dreams can be transformed into the pure appearances of deity and pureland.

In dream practice, inspired by the Buddha when he took parinirvāṇa, the practitioner can put a long piece of kuśa grass under the right side of his body and a short piece of kuśa grass under his head as a symbol of purity for an auspicious blessing. He then sleeps in the parinirvāṇa position and prays to his deity that when he dreams, he will recognize it as a dream. However, there is no benefit to only recognizing the dream if there is no method used to transform its ordinary phenomena into unobscured, pure Buddhafield phenomena. Both recognition and transformation must be accomplished.

We are more likely to recognize that we are dreaming if a dream stirs us deeply. For example, through the fear experienced from a negative, disturbing dream of torment and terror, the mind becomes vividly clear, and it can be recognized that the dream is a dream. In the same way, through the joy experienced from a positive, amazing dream of exaltation and wonder, the mind becomes vividly clear, and it can be recognized that the dream is a dream. Through the circumstance of recognizing either negative or positive dreams as dreams, the practitioner can more easily realize that the dream does not exist anywhere and is only habit.

Because of daytime reality phenomena, dreams seem true. In order not to be trapped in ordinary reality phenomena while dreaming and to develop the confidence of one's own mind, practices are done to train the mind to transform one's own phenomena. In dream practice, human form can be transformed into animal form, animal form into human form, and human form into deity. Countless variations of forms are created and then synthesized into one form, and from one form, countless variations of forms are created again. The practitioner also can freely pass through the elements in dream practice, unobstructedly entering the earth or flying in the sky. When waking practice depends predominantly on the visualization of intangible, pure deity phenomena, then when dreams are recognized as dreams, their forms can be transformed into infinite aspects of wisdom deity. Through realizing that dreams are the pure magic of magic wisdom body's manifestation, all the ordinary dream phenomena of reality can be transformed into the appearance of deity maṇḍala.

Sleeping dream practice and waking dream practice support and depend on each other. It is very important to remember that all the ordinary waking phenomena of reality are like a dream. Without being continuously ensnared by it, all waking and dreaming phenomena are seen as miraculous wisdom deity. Since dream practice develops the practitioner's ability to transform his phenomena, it is especially beneficial for the passage through the transitional state of the juncture between past and future existences. Beings in this state, who have the form of their mental habit, can transform the four name gatherings of feeling, perception, intention, and consciousness into the purelands of the five Dhyāni Buddhas.

The Yoga of the Transmission of Consciousness,
Which Is the Determination of the Path

There are five methods for the transmission of consciousness which accommodate the differences in the realization, practice, and confidence of individual practitioners.

The supreme transmission is for those with keen faculties who have become fully accomplished practitioners with the point of view of deathless great confidence that corresponds to stainless Dharmakāya. This view releases the consciousness from the trap of the karmic body, from the trap of the habit of phenomena, and from the trap of the karmic mind. When a clay pot breaks, the space within the pot joins the space outside, like sky dissolving into sky. Likewise, when the practitioner's last breath is taken and the body is left, without any conception of death, awareness mind is self-enlightened in Dharmakāya.

For practitioners with incisive concentration who have confidence in the visualization and completion stages of practice, there is the transmission of the point of view of insubstantial, pureland exaltation which corresponds to the luminous appearances of Sambhogakāya. When the transitional state of the uncontrived, essential nature opens, awareness mind becomes Sambhogakāya pureland through the power of recognizing wisdom deity, just as the light of the full moon setting on the mountain of the west becomes the light of the sun rising from the mountain of the east.

If, from lack of confidence, one does not become liberated in the transitional state of the uncontrived essential nature, there is the transmission with the point of view of detachment from saṃsāra that corresponds to aimlessly compassionate Nirmāṇakāya. It is for those practitioners who, remembering the precious teachings from their passage through the transitional state of birth and death, are trying to prevent birth in the lower realms and to be born in pureland, with deep, unhesitating, pure faith. Awareness mind is transmitted into Nirmāṇakāya like the return of a conscientious merchant to his own home after accomplishing the great purpose of his journey.

For practitioners with these three points of view, there is no need for the fourth and fifth transmissions of consciousness, which are for those who cannot practice in these ways.

The transmission through the three perceptions is for ordinary beings who have not practiced according to the view of the three kāyas during their lives. In order to complete their practice, they transmit their consciousness with deep faith through their central channel into deity pureland. The central channel is the perception of the path, consciousness is the perception of the eagerly departing guest, and finally, after the last breath, ejection to the pureland is the perception of returning home.

There are many different sādhanas for the transmission through ejection, corresponding to the karmic connections which individuals have to different deity phenomena. The practitioner focuses his practice on the Buddha with whom he has the strongest karmic connection and visualizes himself as an enlightened being in the lineage of that Buddha and his pureland. He visualizes the Buddha above his crown cakra, and he visualizes himself as a deity with a central channel having four characteristics: as straight as a young bamboo shoot, as thin as a lotus petal, as vivid and shining as lacquer, and as clear as the light of a sesame oil lamp. The channel is closed below the navel in order to prevent rebirth in the lower realms and rises up, opening through the crown cakra. Then the essence of consciousness is visualized either as a clear white sphere or as a more elaborate syllable in the heart cakra. With the sound of the Buddha's wisdom syllable of ejection, the practitioner sends his consciousness up the central channel through the opening at his crown cakra into the heart of the Buddha, who is the essence of his root teacher.

After each period of practice, the practitioner returns the consciousness to the heart. Then, in order to make his life long and firm, the root teacher-deity visualized at the crown cakra above the practitioner's head is transformed into the wisdom Buddha of immeasurable life in the lineage of his practice, such as Amitāyus. However, there is actually no contradiction in practicing for long life with any of the aspects of Buddhas, since all Buddhas are indestructible. The practitioner becomes inseparable from the deity. The practitioner then closes the opening at the top of the central channel. This practice of sending the consciousness through the crown cakra into the heart of the Buddha is repeated until there is a sign of accomplishment, such as the crown cakra opening up, emitting fluid, or being able to be penetrated with a piece of kuśa grass. Also, one's teacher can know if the practice has been accomplished through knowing one's experience.

When a sign occurs, it is not necessary to continue to do this practice, but only to retain the phenomena of pureland and to often remember, pray, and offer to one's root teacher. Then, when unavoidable circumstances of death arise, ejection into the pureland is actually performed and accomplished without returning the consciousness to the body as previously practiced, like an arrow shot by a powerful giant that streaks through the sky without ever falling back toward saṃsāra. By this method, the practitioner is reborn in the Nirmāṇakāya pureland of his chosen deity, in order to complete his practice through the blessings of the purelands' Buddhas.

Each of these four methods must be practiced while living in the transitional state of birth and death. The method which is followed depends on the capacity of the practitioner.

The fifth method, the transmission of the compassionate hook, is for those who were unable to practice according to the preceding methods. When they are in the transitional state of dying, they can be guided by highly realized wisdom teachers with great confidence in wisdom mind. These wisdom teachers send the dying being's consciousness into pureland through prayers, visualization, and the actual enactment of ejection, like a loving mother who with great kindness does not allow her child to wander aimlessly through the bustling, chaotic town of saṃsāra, but leads him to her soothing, celestial country.

The Yoga of the Transitional States, Which Is the Joining of the Path

The six yogas and the six transitional states are naturally connected, although they can be taught individually. This is because the phenomena of these practices and states of existence all originate from one mind, as previously mentioned.

By recognizing the actual nature of the appearance of phenomena within any of the transitional states, we can be released from all in-between states to betweenless enlightenment. Everything is a transitional state when the display of stainless Dharmakāya space is not recognized. For those who can practice and become enlightened in this life within the transitional state of birth and death, there is no need for categories of transitional states. But if enlightenment is not attained in the transitional state of birth and death because of karmic obscurations or lack of diligence, then it is important to know that enlightenment can be attained in either the transitional state of the uncontrived essential nature or in the transitional state of the juncture between past and future existences. During either of these two transitional states, whatever practice was done in the transitional state of birth and death can then be accomplished. By realizing that all phenomena are the appearance of deity through accomplishing unity with the deity with whom there is a special karmic connection and a sacred promise to be inseparable, and by seeing all appearances of peaceful and wrathful aspects of phenomena as the display of mind, enlightenment can be attained in either of these transitional states.

The *transitional state of dying* begins with the circumstances that cause death and continues until the karmic airs are completely exhausted. It is the passage from this life to the next state of existence. It is called a transitional state because mind has moved from primordial purity and is wandering in the suffering of the delusion of the habit of reality, unless the potential to return to primordial purity is recognized and accomplished through practice. Its duration depends on the circumstances of death, such as sudden accidents for some and long illnesses for others, which are the consequences of each individual's previously created karmic habit.

Distracted by worldly phenomena, many people misuse good circumstances for practice during their lives. Then, at the time of death, they become anxious and worried. If people have dense, nihilist habits, they will have no idea what to do when death begins. No one will be able to help them, including doctors. Their enemies may wish that they will soon be dead, and their family and friends may hope that they will soon be well, but no one can do anything to make them live forever. Even though they cannot take one single object with them, they still will not be able to abandon their objects of attachment. The six desirable qualities will vanish as their own six senses fade. Finally, the bodies they have cared for and served like gods will become garbage, thrown away in a graveyard.

In the transitional state of dying, many sublime teachers have said we must be like a charming, self-conscious young girl who repeatedly glances at the mirror to make sure of her appearance before leaving the house. We must carefully check that we have completed everything in our lives by making sure that no disorder or difficulties have been left behind for others and that we are not holding on to worldly concerns which could cause attachment that creates future states of ordinary existence. We must especially attend to whatever we are practicing, watching to be sure that we continue to practice with our original determination to have confidence in the ultimate point of view. However much fear or confidence we have is based on this.

At the time of death, it is important not to bring back memories of one's previous life or any phenomena that are connected to a worldly level. It is not beneficial to think about what one has lost and is losing, which can cause the negativity of sadness, unhappiness, or depression. One can lose one's mind to this way of thinking, because it weakens the mind and can cause panic. In general, since the ordinary elements are substantial and diminishing, they do not have any long-lasting power. Therefore, conceptions that are only connected to the ordinary elements cause energy to be depleted. Even if one has some energy left when close to death, worldly thinking will decrease it and can shorten the length of one's life by eating one's energy more quickly, since the mind's turbulence attacks itself. Instead, one must encourage oneself, thinking of all Buddhas or one's own individual wisdom deity. Since Buddha has impenetrable, inconceivable wisdom energy, it is good even for ordinary energy if one is permeated by this blessing through having a stable, determined mind focused on Buddha phenomena. It is unquestionably beneficial for attaining enlightenment.

In the Buddhist tantric medical tradition, it is possible for a doctor to determine if someone is dying by examining his urine and the pulse of his channels. Signs of death can also be identified through many other methods described in inner tantric treatises. The length of life can be measured astrologically, predicted by sublime beings, and known from unusual dreams.

Signs of death can be shown in some common dreams, such as dreams about great change, cleaning that is not related to purification practices, an incurably sick person becoming well, departure, especially toward the south, and other dreams which are explained in tantric texts on dream interpretation. These dreams are especially accurate if they occur at dawn. Positive signs of death can be shown in the uncommon dreams of pure practitioners, such as the appearance of wisdom ḍākinīs coming as guides toward pureland, the appearance of deities, including the particular deity with whom the practitioner has a special connection, the appearance of Buddhas and Bodhisattvas predicting, teaching, and bestowing blessings, or the transformation of the practitioner into his particular deity.

People with a nonspiritual point of view think that when beings die, everything about them ends and is exhausted into nothing. But according to the tantric teachings of Buddhism, death means that although the temporary karmic body finishes, the mind continues.

Beings assume the gross, impure elements of karmic bodies because the original, intangible elements, which are the qualities of wisdom mind, are obscured. This does not mean that wisdom has been weakened, because wisdom can never be weak, but that it has become dormant. It only means that the karmic airs of heavy habits are more apparent to beings with heavy karmic senses, temporarily concealing wisdom light. When beings die, their karmic airs no longer have any gross support because the five skandhas of form, feeling, perception, intention, and consciousness vanish. This vanishing of the skandhas is according to the phenomena of ordinary beings who are dying and become unconscious so that the skandhas disintegrate, which is called death. Wisdom has no unconsciousness. It is always awareness.

Death is actually the dissolution back into the original subtle elements from which the gross outer elements have been created. Since continuous mind exists within the elements, its natural power reappears when the gross elements are released into the natural light elements. At that time, the power of the original, pure, natural wisdom elements is awakened, which demonstrates the intangible existence of the wisdom elements which have been hidden by the gross elements. The gross elements disappear at the time of death because of the emergence of the wisdom airs of the naturally pure elements. From the power of this occurrence, no ordinary elements can remain.

If this natural return to the original elements is not used to recognize the state of the three kāyas, then one goes back again to the samsaric karmic elements. If one can use the dissolution of these samsaric elements into the actual pure elements, death becomes the deathless, pure wisdom appearance of the three kāyas. By accomplishing this, the personal phenomena of samsāra ends. This is the directionless, timeless continuity of wisdom.

At the time of dying, there are signs that the elements are dissolving. Although the stages of dissolution are traditionally described as occurring in a particular sequence, they may also come in other sequences due to variations in the karmic phenomena of each individual. The stages of dissolution can also be described differently according to the phenomena of the elements experienced by the being who is dying. The five inner elements of flesh, fluid, heat, breath, and consciousness can be understood either as dissolving into each other or as dissolving into the five outer elements of earth, water, fire, air, and space. These are not different processes, but only different explanations of the same dissolution. The meaning in each case is that the being's elements are dissolving. Through lack of understanding, beings do not recognize that the impure appearances at the time of death are actually pure, like the pure appearances that arise at other times when the elements dissolve, such as when falling asleep and when practicing.

When death begins, the senses lose their power as the elements dissolve. The earth element, which corresponds to the flesh of the body, dissolves into the water element, which corresponds to the fluid of the body. There is the experience of heaviness and the feeling of not being able to move. As form dissolves into sound, vision diminishes and becomes unclear. The appearance of miragelike shimmering is seen.

The water element dissolves into the fire element, which corresponds to the heat of the body, and there is the experience of dryness and thirst. As sound dissolves into smell, it becomes progressively more difficult to hear. The appearance of smokiness is seen.

The fire element dissolves into the air element, which corresponds to the breath, and there is the experience of extreme coldness as the heat leaves the body and all warmth gathers into the heart. As smell dissolves into taste, the ability to smell is lost. The appearance of very tiny lights like fireflies is seen.

The air element dissolves into the space element, which corresponds to consciousness, and there are more pauses in breathing as inhalation decreases, exhalation increases, and breathing begins to stop. There is the experience of darkness or the feeling of disappearing, until the last breath is taken. As taste dissolves into touch, the ability to taste is lost. The appearance of beaming lamplight is seen.

When consciousness dissolves into space, all gross and subtle grasping ceases. Touch dissolves into consciousness and all perception of feeling ends.

The dissolution of the subtle elements begins when consciousness dissolves into the stage of phenomena. At this time, the white element received from the father's seed, which is the aspect of skillful means, descends into the heart, so that there is the experience of a white appearance like moonlight. Through the return to the basic, pure, original elements, all conceptual obtainments of desire cease and wisdom bliss arises.

After that, the stage of phenomena dissolves into the stage of enhancement. The red element received from the mother's fluid, which is the aspect of wisdom, ascends into the heart, so that there is the experience of a red appearance like sunlight. All conceptual obtainments of aversion cease because of the power at that time of wisdom clarity, and consciousness becomes crystalline.

After that, the stage of enhancement dissolves into the stage of acquirement. The white and red appearances meet in the heart and the phenomena of space dissolve into light. There is an experience like the clear darkness of an unobscured night sky. Conceptionless, luminous wisdom ecstasy occurs and returns into primordial dharmatā. All elements dissolve into the basis of mind. Depending on the individual, there is either a fall into unconsciousness or there is an awakening of awareness. All conceptual obtainments of ignorance cease, and conceptionless wisdom opens.

After that, the stage of acquirement dissolves into luminosity. When lifeholding karmic air has completely separated from the skandhas, primordial, unobstructed space arises like the unobscured dawn sky of autumn, uninfluenced by the red phenomena of sunlight, the white phenomena of moonlight, or the darkness of obscuration. All conceptual obtainments dissolve and the wisdom of self-awareness radiates, free from all mental activities and fabrications. Most beings experience this for at least an instant. At that time, those who have recognized and have the confidence to abide in the luminosity of uncontrived natural mind can instantaneously be liberated into Dharmakāya. All samsaric phenomena are freed into actual parinirvāṇa.

Although the dissolution of the ordinary elements is described in order for the practitioner to be able to identify it, the pith of dissolution is to make the connection with the wisdom elements of the Buddhas. One does not need to concentrate on what happens within the ordinary elements at all, since dissolution happens automatically, but only to remember one's practice and maintain awareness. Even one's awareness is ultimately not dependent on the ordinary elements. As the ordinary elements weaken, it may seem momentarily that one has less concentration because of the habit of using the support of a karmic body and karmic airs for the mind to function, but mind is released from this dependency at death. As the wisdom elements are opened, one's awareness becomes much more powerful and it is much easier to attain the aim of one's practice.

If a practitioner has recognized the luminosity of wisdom space through formless meditation, then there is no more dying according to his actual pure phenomena. As nondualistic mind opens through the circumstance of dying, his awareness is freed by its separation from the five skandhas, and he can recognize that death is itself Dharmakāya. It is said that consciousness dissolves into sky. This does not mean that there is a disappearance into nothingness and that there is no mind. Consciousness becomes cleansed because it is not influenced by the distorted elements, so everything becomes automatically pure. Also, this sky does not mean the objective blue sky of beings' general perception which is made up from the habit of their conceptions and is only an object of mind. It means the indivisibility of stainless space. This is taking the path of transforming death phenomena into Dharmakāya expanse.

So therefore, for supreme practitioners, there is no experience of dissolution at the time of death. They are directly enlightened in Dharmakāya without the interference of the stages of phenomena, enhancement, and acquirement. That is why one Tibetan saint has said, "Death is not death, but is rather enlightening for yogis."

If the practitioner is not liberated at the time of death into Dharmakāya, then he can be liberated if his mind becomes clear in the *transitional state of the uncontrived essential nature,* which is dharmatā, occurring when the mind's inherent natural reflections spontaneously arise. It is called a transitional state because mind has moved from primordial purity and the reflections of the essential nature manifest, unless the potential to return to primordial purity is recognized and attained through practice. Its duration depends on the confidence of the individual in the recognition of mind's essential nature.

After the transitional state of dying, some beings with strong habits go directly to another realm without experiencing the arising of any phenomena of the uncontrived essential nature. For others, this state lasts longer, and phenomena arise in peaceful and wrathful aspects in the form of many different extraordinary, awesome beings and with a variety of sounds. Most beings experience at least a flash of these reflections of their mind.

Those who do not have confidence in wisdom mind miss the opportunity for realization which comes with this display of self-appearance. This is because they perceive these appearances as a separate, objective reality, the same as they did with their habit of reality during previous lives, without recognizing them as the expression of their own mind. Through thinking that these visions are real, they react with fear and lose consciousness. After awakening from this, they begin to take birth in the next life, continuously following after their karmic habit. But if, as a result of the previous experience of his practice of deity visualization, the being who has died recognizes the natural, transparent appearance of the luminosity of dharmatā, he can cut through this circle of ordinary birth and death.

For example, if a mother and child are separated, when they meet again, the child recognizes her and goes directly to her lap without hesitation, joining with her inseparably. The mother is the basis, which is the great, spacious, natural, clear light sky that is pure from the beginningless beginning; the child is the path, which is the recognition through practice of the natural luminosity of self-appearance; and the result is their inseparability. In this way, the uncontrived essential nature can be transformed into the five Dhyāni Buddha families' measureless pure maṇḍala of Sambhogakāya radiance.

If the practitioner is not liberated in the Sambhogakāya clear light, then he can be liberated by recognition of and confidence in the Sambhogakāya phenomena of the self-manifesting array of peaceful and wrathful deities in the *transitional state of the junction between past and future existences*. This state follows the transitional state of the uncontrived essential nature and precedes the next life. It occurs if the phenomena of the transitional state of the uncontrived essential nature are not recognized as the display of mind. Its characteristics come partly from the phenomena of the previous life's habits, and partly from the phenomena of the future life's signs. It is called a transitional state because mind has moved from primordial purity and is wandering in the suffering of the delusion of the habit of reality, unless the potential to return to primordial purity is recognized and attained through practice. Its duration depends on each individual's previously created karmic habit.

From the force of negative karma, some unfortunate beings do not experience either this or the previous transitional state, taking birth directly in the lower realms after death. From the force of practice, some beings do not experience either of these transitional states because they are enlightened directly into Dharmakāya at the time of death. But ordinary beings usually pass through this in-between period and, if they were not able to liberate themselves through Sambhogakāya appearances in the previous transitional state, they have another opportunity for liberation in this state.

During the transitional state of the juncture between past and future existences, ordinary beings usually experience confusion and doubt about whether or not death has actually occurred. They retain a mental habit body. They may make frustrated attempts to communicate with family and friends who are their objects of attachment remaining in the transitional state of birth and death, but they do not respond. By examining their mental body, the beings in this transitional state can see that it is shadowless and leaves no footprints. When they understand that they no longer have their previous physical body and have died, fear increases and grows even greater with the knowledge that another rebirth is approaching over which they have no control. Beings can become immersed in their own turmoil, caught between their attachment to the old phenomena of many previous habits and the disturbance of what is mentally experienced as the new phenomena of their future life.

When superior practitioners who have confidence die, the superior way to attain enlightenment is to liberate themselves immediately into Dharmakāya through the recognition that any appearances which arise are not true. When practitioners with intermediate experience die, the intermediate way to attain enlightenment is to liberate the appearances of the uncontrived essential nature by visualizing Sambhogakāya appearances of the maṇḍala of the deity of their personal practice. Those who cannot be liberated through either of these means can pray to their deity in order to be liberated into the pureland of the deity to complete their practice and become enlightened.

If death has not been transformed into Dharmakāya, or if the appearances of the uncontrived essential nature have not been transformed into Sambhogakāya pure appearances, then the transitional state of birth and death can be transformed into Nirmānakāya. In order to complete their practice, beings can be born in the immeasurable lands of Nirmānakāya, where Buddhas are emanating and teaching, until the three kāyas become inseparable, which is the state of Buddhas. In the same way as a water channel which has broken apart needs to be rejoined to allow the water to flow continuously, when one fortunate, karmic body has been exhausted, another must be taken in order for the main channel of practice to be continued until its completion. A new form can be assumed with the pure intention and prayer that the rest of one's practice will be accomplished through a precious human rebirth. The seed syllable of the deity with whom one is karmically connected through previous practice is visualized, inseparable from the essence of one's mind. A mother who will be a support to Dharma is chosen, and her womb is transformed into the intangible, wisdom design of the pureland and palace of this deity. With deity's phenomena, awareness is sustained within this container as the senses begin to form. Because it is blessed by wisdom deity's phenomena, even the physical body which is born has clearer senses than the body of an ordinary being, and many auspicious signs appear.

The *transitional state of dreaming* is the interval between ordinary waking phenomena and deep, dreamless sleep, in which the mental habit body of sentient beings continues to exist. It is called a transitional state because mind has moved from primordial purity and is wandering in the suffering of the delusion of the habit of reality, unless the potential to return to primordial purity is recognized and attained through practice. Its duration depends on each individual's previously created karmic habit.

No matter where one is born, if one has nihilist habits, one moves meaninglessly from life to life between ordinary consciousness and ordinary dreaming. Since ordinary mind is perpetually dualistic, endless suffering can be caused by just one being with a fragmented mind who does not believe in practicing the Buddha's teachings. Even one single mind in one single body sleeping in one single bed can create countless ordinary dream beings and countless ordinary dream objects. Since ordinary waking time is suspended, we can dream about many different phenomena and occurrences within one short moment, or we can dream about very few phenomena and occurrences during one long moment. But even when we seemingly have very few dream phenomena, they are actually countless, since our deluded phenomena started many lives ago, even though we do not know when it was.

Wherever there is ordinary waking, there is ordinary dreaming, and wherever there is ordinary dreaming, there is ordinary waking. Wherever there are both ordinary waking and ordinary dreaming, there is ignorance, which is the way of ordinary sentient beings. The only release from this is through belief in the Buddha's true teachings and through trying to practice with the wisdom deities of our karmic connection, inseparable with great emptiness.

We may not pay attention to our dreams if we only believe in waking phenomena through our nihilist habit. But even if dreams do not seem real while we are awake, through the habit of waking reality, dreams seem real while we are dreaming. We cannot ignore dreams as long as we are still affected by going back and forth between unpleasant and pleasant phenomena which produce unhappiness and happiness. As long as we have dualistic mental activity from grasping at experiences, dreams affect the expression of continuous mind within our phenomena and influence our energy.

Negativity and confusion can be created through unpleasant dreams, causing mental disturbances in exactly the same way as these disturbances happen when we are awake. Just as waking phenomena appear in our dreams, these dreamtime mental disturbances can in turn affect our waking phenomena. For instance, a nightmare we may have as a result of waking phenomena can cause negative feelings that affect us after we have awakened. In this way, waking and dreaming can incessantly influence each other and create the seeds of mental problems. If unhappiness arises continuously, it can create bad feelings and negative energy which interfere with the life force, causing mental problems that are very difficult to treat with substantial means such as medicines and sophisticated verbiage. Instead, we should practice with the optimistic belief that we can create positive dreams, which influences both our dreams and daytime phenomena positively.

The essence of dream practice is to see that waking phenomena are the same as the illusory qualities of dreams. Then, through practice, we can try to introduce the clear space of luminosity into dreaming, as described earlier in the yoga of dreams. Like lighting a torch in a dark hall, we must have awareness. When the outwardly distracting conceptions of the six senses are dissolving inwardly into sleep and mindfulness has not yet been lost in unconsciousness, if we can recognize the pure, untarnished nature of unending wisdom, it is luminosity. We must try to remain in this luminosity as long as possible. We must try to change heavy, negative dreams into light, positive dreams, and gradually dissolve both negative and positive dreams into stainless, luminous space.

If we can practice like this continuously, our habit of ordinary waking phenomena will be transformed into pure noble habit. This pure noble habit continuously increases our natural, intangible energy so that it can blossom into intangible wisdom energy, and when we sleep we have fewer and fewer obscured, distorted dreams. Instead, we dream of pure Buddhafields where we continue to pray, offer, and visualize. We can see Buddha's wisdom form, we can hear Buddha's wisdom teaching, and we can feel Buddha's wisdom blessing.

Many wonderful dreams can arise by practicing in this way. Then, as our noble dream habit increases, it influences our ordinary waking phenomena. If we also develop our waking practice with tangible, sacred images or intangible, visualized images of deity, purify our obscurations and habits, and make accumulations of merit and wisdom, then our noble waking phenomena and our noble dream phenomena will enhance each other. Gradually, we will no longer discriminate between the phenomena of noble dreaming and noble waking. Through our dream practice, when we die, there is no more death, there is no more birth, and there is no more deep dreamless sleep.

As in any Buddhist practice, the aim of dream practice is to reach enlightenment. With the recognition and confidence that come from continuous practice between waking dreaming and sleeping re-dreaming, the border between waking and dreaming is erased into the unending continuity of pure wisdom appearance and stainless emptiness. Without realizing the point of view of great emptiness, there is no way to dissolve the changing phenomena of being awake and dreaming. Either in daytime or dreamtime, the ultimate essence of any practice is the point of view, recognized through the guidance of our guardian wisdom teacher and then used with practice.

The *transitional state of meditation* begins when practitioners recognize natural, nondualistic wisdom mind and continues through their practice of meditation until they reach enlightenment. It is called a transitional state because the movement away from primordial purity and back to primordial enlightenment creates a path between the primordial purity of the basis and the primordial purity of the result of enlightenment, which is inexpressible, boundless unity. Since there is a path, it automatically means that there is a transitional state between the basis and result. Its duration depends on when the result of practice is reached. This depends on whether the faculties of the individual disciple are dull and slow, intermediate and gradual, or keen and simultaneous; whether his mind has intellectual understanding or the experience of recognition; the level of instructions he is given; which teachings he practices; how much practice he does; the development of his practice; and the realization and skillfull means of the teacher.

According to the lower yānas, basic mind holds the essence of the cause and result of all false appearance, like a seed from which fruit ripens, and it is the support of all flawless appearances, like precious medicine which may be found even within a poison container. According to the teachings of the higher yānas, basic mind is pure from the beginningless beginning and is the nature of enlightenment, so it is called the basis of the mind of enlightenment.

For those who cannot realize enlightened self-appearance awareness mind through the teachings of the effortless Great Perfection and by practice on the path that is itself self-liberating, the correct point of view has to be established with effort to attain meditation's states of tranquil stillness and sublime seeing. This is supported by abandoning the five faults of laziness, forgetfulness, dullness and elation, unclear intention, and excessive intensity, and applying their eight antidotes. The antidotes for laziness are faith, attentiveness, diligence, and refinement of the mind; the antidote for forgetfulness is mindfulness; the antidote for dullness and elation is continuous awareness; the antidote for unclear intention is watchfulness; and the antidote for excessive intensity is equanimity.

Dharmabhadra, All-Knowing Noble Appearance, gave instructions on how to practice with mind using the following methods:

The monkey must be tied. Since the consciousness of mind is like a wild monkey who does not do what needs to be done and who does what should not be done, we must tie this monkey mind's consciousness with the rope of mindfulness.

The cat must be leashed. Although a cat may seem to be smooth, soft, and gentle, it steals the lives of other beings. Likewise, although the movement of mind's passions is very subtle, it is the seed of ego in the basis of mind which raises all false samsaric appearances. Instead of letting this happen, the passions must be leashed with the cord of egoless realization.

The collections of an empty, ruined house must be destroyed. Attachment to the five aggregates has no benefit and no essence, and must be destroyed by the point of view of skylike realization, which always releases any obstructions.

The windows must be shut. The ordinary five consciousnesses move with distraction from the five senses toward outer objects. Instead, the mind must be taken inward, disciplined, and controlled so that it is undisturbed by outer phenomena.

The king's treasury must be opened. Just as a king's treasury may contain both poisons and priceless jewels, the potentials of both false appearances and desireless wisdom appearances exist in the consciousness of basic mind. To be wise about this source of immeasurable phenomena, we must uncover and understand the characteristics of basic mind through practice.

There are many traditions which teach the basis of meditation and describe categories and stages of practice and realization, such as the ten stages that depend on the Sūtra system and the five main paths that depend on the Vajrayāna system.

The categories of the five main paths begin with the path of accumulation, which includes studying with a sublime teacher in order to understand and establish the correct point of view, purifying obscurations, and accumulating merit. The path of joining is the beginning of recognizing point of view and uniting with the path of sublime seeing. It is like the dawn which comes from the sun rays of sublime seeing's wisdom. As unborn natural mind manifests, it is experienced as insubstantial form which elevates the practitioner on the path of joining to the recognition of sublime seeing. The path of sublime seeing does not depend on any method, and is actually seeing the inconceivable, stainless, essential nature of wisdom mind. The path of meditation is the continuous practice of the states of *the wisdom of abiding in nonduality* and *the wisdom after attaining nonduality* until they are inseparable. Then all practice is exhausted into the path of no more learning.

Even though the Buddha's teachings have one essence, they are infinite and always a reflection of individuals' capacities, which are always different from each other. In any case, it is the personal teacher's responsibility to teach in a way that adapts to each student's faculties. Although each of the systems that define the borders of what can be recognized within meditation practice cannot be mentioned here, the basic methods, categories, and teachings of meditation can be synthesized from these traditions in a simple way into form meditation and formless meditation.

When we start to meditate, emptiness must be made into form. We use form in order to see the manifestation of primordial, natural wisdom appearance and to recognize emptiness, which is indivisible from wisdom appearance. Since we have already created the countless forms of existence, we have to concentrate on form in order to see that it is empty. It may seem that it is not right to do this because we will become attached to the object of our concentration, but it is actually correct. In practice, we have to start with attachment to a target or a focus, such as a pure, light, positive object of inspiration. Through sustaining this attachment, the natural quality of mind can be seen, from which nonattachment is born.

Form meditation is practiced in the Sūtra system by concentrating one-pointedly on the mind. Because it appears that there is no specific object of concentration and focus, it may seem as if there is no form. But until dualistic mind finishes, there is the object of mind and the subject that watches it. As long as we are focusing, there is still empty, formless form until all dualistic habit of concentrator and concentration vanishes.

Some people are only interested in practicing formless meditation. But it can cause dullness to practice without any positive wisdom Buddha phenomena, just sitting without praying and without any point of view. Therefore, formless meditation must be done with mindfulness, clear awareness, and the instruction of wisdom teachers. The key is that wisdom is always inseparable from its qualities of undeluded awareness. In formless meditation, concentration is used especially to focus in order to purify our habit of scattered thoughts.

To reach mind's formlessness, there are many methods of focus that use an ordinary form such as a pebble or an ordinary process such as breathing. Also, extraordinary form can be used, such as breathing with the recitation of the three-seed-syllable mantra of wisdom vajra body, speech, and mind, or such as a deity's image, including that of Buddha Śakyamuni. As it says in *The King of Sublime Samādhi Sūtra*:

> Stainless, golden-colored body,
> Always exquisite lord of the universe;
> Whoever beholds this
> Is in Bodhisattva's samādhi.

These methods are used to establish tranquil stillness, to realize actual, natural, sublime, inexpressible wisdom insight which is the blossoming of Buddha nature, and to continuously progress on the path of wisdom qualities until enlightenment is reached.

It is not necessary to think that deities and prayers are missing in formless meditation, because all Buddhas and all deities are contained in the formless state of wisdom awareness, since all Buddhas' utmost body is sole Dharmakāya. That is why it is said in the *Guhyasamāja*:

> If you wish to attain supreme enlightenment,
> Do not read volumes of scriptures
> And do not circumambulate stupas.
> If you do, it is very difficult to attain enlightenment.

This does not mean to remain in a nihilist, nothingness negation, but to abide in the state of nondualistic awareness mind which connects to stainless Dharmakāya.

It is very important in meditation that, through mindfulness, the conceptions of dualistic mind which are the basis of saṃsāra are not allowed to settle. Obviously arising gross conceptions are easy to recognize, like a seagull that is caught by a crocodile. However, it is very difficult to recognize hidden, sleeping, subtle conceptions, like a seagull flying in space above the sea whose shadow is being chased by a crocodile in the water below. This was mentioned by Omniscient Nobility of Appearance in *Entering the Tradition of the Great Vehicle,* so that apparent conceptions and dormant conceptions could be recognized.

Because of the ordinary, samsaric habits of many lives, the mind cannot settle and continues to move even in meditation. As Buddha said in *The Ocean of Wisdom Sūtra*:

> Ocean of Wisdom! If you look at a great ocean from a long
>   distance, it is not moving.
> But if you go close to the ocean, it is moving.
> Likewise, the samādhi of all Bodhisattvas is seemingly
>   unmoving.
> But if seen from the wisdom eyes of Buddha, it is not
>   unmoving.

It is necessary to have mindfulness without contradiction between form meditation, such as the visualization of deities, and formless meditation, such as the samādhi free from mental activity. By recognizing the ultimate indivisibility of form and formless practice, ordinary, samsaric habits are not created but diminish so that the unmoving state of Buddhahood can be attained.

Like balancing a vessel full of water, the balance of concentration must be exact until mindfulness is transformed into the unintentional, complete, timeless awakening of wisdom mind. This is the great continuity of knowing the view of the Great Perfection, which, like the sky, is beyond all movement, unaffected by the motion of a garuḍa's wings, blowing winds, or anything whatsoever. In the balance of great, stainless sole mind, there is no duality of subject and object, so there is no cause for the passions to arise. Since there are no passions, there is no karma. Since there is no karma, there is no samsāra. There is only free, self-manifesting compassion guiding all sentient beings. As it says in *The Sūtra of Increasing Faith*:

> There is no wisdom other than the natural passions,
> So the passions themselves are wisdom.

This means that the passions themselves do not have a substantial existence anywhere. There is only the clarity of the awareness of awakened mind, which is the essence of the passions. Also, in *The Sūtra of the Display of the Manifestation of Mañjuśrī,* it says:

Sister, like this, for example,
Wherever the sky is burning, the sky cannot be burned
     by fire.
Sister, likewise, like this,
Whatever is naturally clear light cannot be obscured by any
     sudden, temporary passions that arise.

Without the passions, wisdom cannot be found. So therefore, it is said in the sūtras:

Thus, the excrement of townspeople
Is beneficial as fertilizer for the people of Sugarfield.
Likewise, the fertilizing passions of Bodhisattvas
Are beneficial for accomplishing the state of enlightenment.

Meditation and realization come easily for those with fortunate karma and gifted capacities for recognizing wisdom mind, so that any tradition can be practiced directly, including the high teachings of the Great Perfection. But since it is rare to be so gifted, the mind must first be made calm and clean. If a pond is stirred up with a stick, nothing can be seen in its clouded water; but if it is left to settle, it becomes clear so that the pristine nature of the water can be seen. Likewise, we practice by settling and clarifying the mind to establish the state of tranquil stillness.

There are three stages of tranquil stillness. In the beginning, conceptions come conspicuously and continuously like a waterfall's rough and unceasing descent, with one conception following after another. This does not mean that the mind has become more turbulent due to meditation, but only that before the meditator began to meditate, he did not notice his ordinary mind's disturbance because he was distracted toward outer objects. So although it may seem that conceptions have increased, it is only that the meditator becomes more aware of his conceptions by watching them through concentrating one-pointedly on the mind. Still, he should meditate continuously, without stopping from frustration.

In the intermediate stage of tranquil stillness, the mind becomes like the lightly rippling waves of a flowing river, as gross conceptions become more subtle from watching the mind. Thoughts decrease, the mind becomes more serene, and the meditator becomes happy to meditate.

Finally, tranquil stillness becomes like a calm ocean, undisturbed by waves of thoughts. Many experiences arise. The body becomes extremely comfortable, and the meditator is sometimes blissful, sometimes clear, sometimes without thought, and sometimes may not even notice the change between night and day. Since these are extraordinary culminations for the meditator, it is possible to make the error of grasping at these experiences, which can cause attachment and self-righteous ego that can lead to rebirth in the higher samsaric god realms. So, at this time, it is important for the meditator to discuss his experiences with a wisdom teacher who can untie and release him from this mistaken direction and put him on the flawless path of enlightenment.

For many meditators, it is difficult to make the mind clear and pristine in the samādhi of stillness due to the habits of many lives. In order to make the mind settle in stillness, they should visualize Buddha in front of them. As Mipham Rinpoche taught, in order to dispel dullness and to attain the sublime quality of wisdom, the meditator should focus the mind toward the natural, inconceivable top of Buddha's crown. In order to attain great merit and reach flawless ecstasy, the meditator should focus toward the precious treasure of crystal, snow-colored hair circling to the right and emanating light in the space between Buddha's refined eyebrows. In order to benefit worldly beings, the meditator should focus toward the three beautiful lines adorning Buddha's supreme, sacred Dharma conch shell-like throat, which is the source of the great sound of Dharma and the origin of the sixty branches of melodious speech. In order to dispel elation and attain firmness of samādhi, the meditator should focus toward the appearance of interlacing light that is a sign of the unending perfection of Buddha's wisdom heart. These methods can be practiced according to the condition of the meditator's mind.

By recognizing that the essence of all appearances is unconditioned, nondualistic wisdom mind, the state of sublime seeing is attained. It is released from all dualistic projections and never causes
delusion, which is the seed of saṃsāra. Even after attaining this state,
it is necessary to increase it with concentration until it is completely
accomplished and we effortlessly remain in Buddha's wisdom mind.
According to the wisdom of the path of enlightenment, we increase
wisdom from the qualities of natural mind through learning and practice so that we are not affected by samsaric phenomena. Then we
transform this wisdom of the path into the omniscient state of wisdom, which is beyond basis, path, and result.

Until we attain this state, which we are developing through
meditation, we must be aware of possible mistakes in order to purify
them. There are three faults that cause the obscuration of tranquil
stillness. If the mind is distracted outwardly, it will not be clear, the
same as the light of a lamp that is blown by outer wind. If the mind
is blocked by not having self-awareness with mindfulness, it will not
be clear, the same as the light of a lamp with a faulty wick that will
either flicker or die, unable to shine smoothly or illuminate continuously. So, there should not be distraction toward outer phenomena
or supression of the radiant, natural mindfulness that arises. Also, if
one concentrates with the rigid focus of grasping mind, inconceivable
samādhi may not be seen. This causes fragmented contemplation, the
same as the water drops of a leak that fall one after another in the
same place and in the same form. The antidote to these three faults is
mindfulness.

There are three faults that cause the obscuration of sublime
seeing. By separating from the realization of the egolessness of
phenomena, one is distracted by whatever phenomena arise when
meditating in samādhi. This causes the emergence of a possessor of
phenomena and prevents liberation. Due to not understanding that
all phenomena come from interdependent circumstances, whatever is
thought is always false. Falling to either of the two extremes of existence and nonexistence prevents seeing the equanimity of wisdom

mind. If there is a limitation of knowing samādhi, one cannot open toward vast awareness mind, like birds that are obstructed from flying by being in a dark room and only circle in one small place.

There are three faults that cause the obscuration of pure effort. Not moving from an old path or not making effort to find a new sublime path is like a baby bird that does not want to abandon its old nest or try a new flight into the sky. Not making effective effort due to following an obscured path causes the loss of concentration in samādhi, which is like shooting an arrow toward a fallen target. Falling to the extreme of excessive grasping at the clarity of mind causes the mind to be unbalanced, the same as when a person who is overly distracted toward objects becomes disturbed through elation.

There are three faults that cause the obscuration of pure samādhi. These are the desire to have many experiences, the desire to have prescience, and the desire to perform miracles. Each conceals the essence of samādhi, which is to attain enlightenment. Those who have these faults are like some farmers who keep many young cows with the main intention of making butter, but through too much desire for using milk and yogurt, they have nothing left for making the essence of butter.

There are three faults that cause the obscuration of mindfulness. These are feeling that one has attained supreme enlightenment, being attached to one's own self-righteous point of view with pride, and having contempt for the points of view of others. Actual, pure mindfulness comes from depending on Buddha's teachings, on their commentaries in the sástras of sublime beings, and on all teachers who can show practitioners the meaning of these teachings. All of these depend on having pure perception with mindfulness. Whenever this pure perception with mindfulness is lost, the main path of mindfulness is lost. For example, if a spoiled son of an aristocratic lineage of ministers forgets his qualities of nobility and acts crudely, his vulgarity will increase and he will lose the power of his lineage.

Whenever one does one's main practice with an awakened mind, either with visualization or with formlessness, it must be understood that the pith of practice is totally insubstantial. If one is still attached to creating elaborate, substantial virtue with an intention based on believing in a tangible reality, such as by reading and writing about many intellectual ideas, it may cause obstacles for one's main practice. Samādhi has no divisions, but this attachment can cause walls which create obscurations, so that one goes from one wall of cognitive obscurations to another. If one is attracted to sophisticated activities, whenever one does actual practice, one must not think about creating more complicated virtue with dualistic intention. All virtue is automatically contained within abiding in a vast point of view.

Whatever practice is done must be permeated with the point of view of great stainless space, which is the supreme consort of Samantabhadra and the wisdom mother of all Buddhas. As it is said in the teaching of *The Contemplation of Enlightened Bodhicitta*:

> If it is not permeated by Kuntuzangmo, even virtuous, noble
> activity becomes the activity of demons and is finally
> exhausted.
> If it is permeated by Kuntuzangmo, even the activity of
> demons becomes the activity of enlightenment.

It is also important to understand that once having entered meditation practice, there are the two experiences of the wisdom of abiding in nonduality and the wisdom after attaining nonduality, which continue as long as we have the habit of duality from wandering in saṃsāra for many lives. Two different kinds of beings do not experience these states. Those who do not practice do not experience the wisdom of abiding in nonduality because they are not meditating. Also, for those who are already enlightened like Buddha beyond the stage of practice, the wisdom of abiding in nonduality and the wisdom after attaining nonduality are inseparable, so not even their names exist.

Whenever we are in the wisdom of abiding in nonduality, whether we are using Vairocana's seven-pointed posture, the posture of resting in natural mind, or just a relaxed posture, we should try to stay in great stainless space. The equanimity of this state is sometimes thought of as a scale balancing equal weights, but it is not a balance between two things. It is the balance of nonduality, which is vast, open oneness, like sky. When there is nothing to balance, it is the balance of abiding in sole, awareness mind, which is called the natural, great balance of samādhi in the teaching of Mahāsandhi. Whenever we move from this state to the wisdom after attaining nonduality, we should not let ourselves be influenced by our previous habit of reality.

Deities are not objects of reality, but intangible light, yet grasping mind can lure the practitioner into trying to seize this light with the attachment of wanting deities to come or to stay in reality. When deities appear, it is important not to grasp at them.

Clinging to the reality of phenomena is released by seeing the illusory untruth of phenomena. This illusory aspect is recognized predominantly from the experience of emptiness, and the quality of unobstructedness becomes the afterglow of its afterappearance.

Until enlightenment, there is always dualistic habit. When Bodhisattvas are in the state of the wisdom of abiding in nonduality, they do not have any habit of reality as other beings do. But when they are in the state of the wisdom after attaining nonduality, there is still the residue of some dualistic habit in the echo of clinging to illusion, although it is immediately transformed through meditation into nondualistic mind. For practitioners, when former heavy habits arise, they are purified by new light habits so that habit can be transcended. When all dualistic habits have almost vanished, there is not even the name of illusory phenomena. So, although there is at first attachment to illusory phenomena, it becomes less and less until there is no difference between illusory phenomena and emptiness.

There are many systems to define the stages of experience which come from the wisdom of abiding in nonduality and the wisdom after attaining nonduality. However much the practitioner can stay in the wisdom of abiding in nonduality, his experience of the wisdom after attaining nonduality becomes automatically that much more light,

pure, and vast because it is influenced by the power of the spaciousness of the wisdom of abiding in nonduality. Until all dual habits have
vanished, we must continuously try to purify all habitual divisions,
including the one between the wisdom of abiding in nonduality and
the wisdom after attaining nonduality. Then, the appearances of the
wisdom after attaining nonduality become more and more vast until
there is no distance or pause between them.

If natural mind is introduced directly, it is not necessary to discriminate between the stages of meditation. Because natural mind is
unending, phenomena cannot end, appearing inseparably with emptiness mind. Since phenomena are self-manifesting, unobstructed appearances always arise inseparably with emptiness. The equanimity
of the state of the wisdom of abiding in nonduality, which originates
predominantly from emptiness, and the phenomena of the state of
the wisdom after attaining nonduality, which originates predominantly from the unobstructed array of self-revelation, cannot be separated. They become one taste, divisionless, clear space.

Since points of view, methods, and individual capacities are different, experiences and qualities that arise from practice vary. Those
with a dull capacity may stay within one stage of practice for a long
time, while those with an intermediate capacity may gradually move
from one stage to another. Those with a keen capacity lift toward
more pure experience more quickly as a result of their previous
karma.

Even though journeying on the same road toward the same
destination, all travelers do not arrive at the same time. A slower
traveler can take a long time to go from one place to another. Over
the same distance, another traveler with a faster method can finish
more quickly. The fastest traveler can fly the same distance within an
instant, finishing before the other travelers, even if he started after
them. Also, although one traveler may appear to be starting later
than another, he may have started earlier, just as a practitioner with a
gifted mind from the practice of previous lives may be continuing on
his former path which joins this life's practice, and may accomplish

his aim quickly. Only sublime beings can know which practitioner can go farthest and fastest by seeing the energy of his karma, intention, faith, the support of the vehicle he follows, and the practice he is doing.

Although stages of practice, such as the five paths and the ten stages, are defined in many texts in both the causal and result vehicles, there are not any stages in the state of the wisdom of abiding in nonduality since it is the sustainment of nondualistic mind. Stages only exist in the state of the wisdom after attaining nonduality. Then experiences, stages, and paths are described because of impure phenomena which still come in this state. As the ordinary phenomena of its afterimages become less and less, the pure, light quality of natural wisdom appearance becomes more and more vast. Then, just as a puddle gradually diminishes when the sun continuously shines on it until the wetness totally evaporates and it is gone, when confidence in the wisdom of abiding in nonduality increases and nondualistic mind becomes steady, the wisdom after attaining nonduality is permeated with the power of the blessing of the wisdom of abiding in nonduality and it is gone.

If the Hīnayāna tradition is followed, the wisdom after attaining nonduality brings detachment from and weariness of saṃsāra and inspires us to increase the state of the wisdom of abiding in nonduality. This subdues all passions that create saṃsāra, leading to the arhat state of enlightenment. If the Mahāyāna tradition is followed, all phenomena are seen as illusory in the wisdom after attaining nonduality. This causes detachment from reality and inspires us to increase illusory compassion for illusory beings who are wandering with reality-thinking perception within illusory phenomena, leading to Buddha's Dharmakāya and Rūpakāya enlightenment. If the inner Vajrayāna tradition is followed, all appearances are seen as pure, magic wisdom deity in the wisdom after attaining nonduality. This is the inspiration for using the deity result as the path, to create wisdom maṇḍala leading to Vajradhāra enlightenment. Especially in the teachings of the Great Perfection, it is not even necessary to conceive of stages, since all stages can be simultaneously accomplished within the meditator's mind.

The three kinds of ignorance are purified through the recognition of wisdom awareness. When beginningless purity is recognized, the ignorance of the possessor is dispelled. When spontaneous self-appearance is recognized as one's own display of the manifestation of unobstructed, beginningless purity, inherent ignorance is dispelled. When one's spontaneous self-phenomena are recognized as selfless, all-naming ignorance is dispelled. Then, the source of saṃsāra has been uprooted.

We try to purify all duality until there is no difference between the wisdom of abiding in nonduality and the wisdom after attaining nonduality. One who can practice like this until attaining enlightenment is called a continuous river yogi. Then there is no division between appearances, which are the inexhaustible wisdom appearances of Sambhogakāya and Nirmānakāya, and stainless emptiness, which is Dharmakāya. There is only one divisionless, unending wisdom maṇḍala.

The precious teachings of the effortless Great Perfection are given especially to those who have the most gifted capacity, deepest devotion, no hesitation, and a teacher who holds its pure lineage. The practice of the perfectly accomplished teaching which establishes the great stainless emptiness of Dharmakāya is the natural revelation of cutting through all substantial and insubstantial phenomena. This is taught in *The Precious Three Verses That Strike the Essence,* which reveals the deep meaning of how to recognize the face of self-awareness wisdom mind, decide that there is nothing more than that to do, and have confidence in abiding in self-freedom. The practice to establish the uncontrived, spontaneous, luminous appearance of natural Buddhas is through the natural revelation of passing simultaneously to the direct, clear light manifestation of Buddhas, which is Sambhogakāya and Nirmānakāya, through direct transmission. This is especially for those who want to enlighten in this life through dharmatā phenomena, without the delay of having a different experience after death of a transitional state of the uncontrived essential nature. The four appearances of experience which are accomplished through this practice are the intangible appearance of the uncontrived essential nature, the appearance of the development of pure experience, the accomplishment of the display of awareness mind, and the complete appearance of the uncontrived essential nature. The great yogi either abides in the youthful vessel body whose self-illumination is like the inwardly dwelling prism of a stainless crystal, or transforms into intangible, miraculous, rainbow wisdom body for the benefit of all beings. Then, like many sublime saints and the vajramaster Padmasambhava, his intangible appearance manifests as a guide for tangible beings to lead them toward the inexhaustible qualities of intangible, luminous Buddhafields.

Glossary

ālaya (Kun.gzhi). The basis of saṃsāra and nirvāṇa which is not unobscured; the basis of mind.

Amitāyus (Tshe.dpag.med). The deity of deathlessness.

arhat (dGra.bchom.pa). One who has attained the state of the purification of the passions.

Ārya Tārā ('Phags.ma sGrol.ma). The sublime goddess Tārā.

bardo (Bar.do). A transitional state of existence; any phenomena that exist other than primordial, stainless awareness.

Bodhisattva (Byang.chhub sems.dpa'). Compassionate sublime being.

bodhi tree (Byang.chhub shing). The tree of enlightenment.

Buddha; Buddhas (Sangs.rgyas). Fully enlightened beings.

Buddha families (Sangs.rgyas kyi rigs). Lineages of Buddhas, including the Buddha family, Vajra family, Ratna family, Padma family, and Karma family. Each of these five families of Buddhas has countless Buddhas, and all of them are supreme Buddhas.

Buddhafield (Zhing.khams). The pure, dustless land of enlightened beings.

Buddhahood (Sangs.rgyas kyi go.'phang). Full enlightenment.

Buddha nature (bDe.gshegs snying.po). Unconditioned wisdom mind.

cakra ('Khor.lo). Wheel.

chhikha bardo ('Chhi.kha bar.do). The transitional state of dying.

chhöku ngowo'i takpa (Chhos.sku ngo.bo'i rtag.pa). The essential permanence of Dharmakāya, which is the unobscured purity of emptiness that cannot be affected by anything.

chhonyid bardo (Chhos.nyid bar.do). The transitional state of the uncontrived essential nature which is dharmatā.

dākinī (mKha'.'gro.ma). Skygoer; the display of wisdom coming and going in dharmadhātu, yet not remaining anywhere.

dharma (Chhos). The holding of phenomena, either samsaric appearance or the wisdom energy of enlightenment.

dharmadhātu (Chhos.dbyings). Immeasurable, stainless space.

Dharmakāya (Chhos.sku). Completely pure formless form.

dharmatā (Chhos.nyid). The uncontrived essential nature.

Dhyāni Buddhas (Sangs.rgyas kyi rigs). Supreme wisdom Buddha families.

ganacakra (Tshogs kyi 'khor.lo). The vehicle of offerings according to the special pujas of the inner tantric tradition.

gandharva (Dri.za). A kind of supernatural being.

garuḍa (Bya.khyung). A supernatural bird which is beyond the conception of nihilist reality, but exists for those who believe in the infinite phenomena of saṃsāra and nirvāṇa, as Buddha revealed according to the different realms of beings.

Guhyasamāja (gSang.ba 'dus.pa). The gathering of the essence of the teachings of the inconceivable secret phenomena of enlightenment of the Vajrayāna tradition.

guru (bLa.ma). Vajramaster, who is in Nirmanakāya's land and guides toward Sambhogakāya and Dharmakāya.

Hīnayāna (Theg.pa dman.pa). The inferior vehicle of Buddhism.

kāyas (sKu.) The aspects of the inconceivable qualities of Buddhas.

kriyā tantra (Bya.rgyud). The yoga of purity.

Kuntuzangmo (Kun.tu.bzang.mo; Samantabhadri). The stainless, inconceivable nature.

kuśa. A kind of special, clean grass which Buddha Śakyamuni used, symbolic of purity.

longku gyunkyi tagpa (Longs.sku rgyun.gyi rtag.pa). The continuous permanence of the immeasurable pure appearances of Sambhogakāya.

Lumbini. The birthplace of Buddha Śakyamuni and one of the four great holy places of Buddha Śakyamuni.

Mahāmudrā (Phyag.rgya chhen.po). Great gesture.

Mahāsandhi (rDzogs.pa chhen.po). The wisdom teaching of the Great Perfection.

Mahāsiddha (Grub.chhen). Great saint.

mahāyoga (rNal.'byor chhen.po). The path of the union of phenomena and emptiness, to attain the result of the union of Vajradhara.

Maitreya (Byams.pa). The future Buddha who is now in Tuṣita Heaven.

maṇḍala (dKyil. 'khor). Immeasurable existence and wisdom energy.

Mandarava. The princess who was the consort of Guru Rinpoche and the daughter of the King of Zahor.

Mantrayāna (sNgags kyi theg.pa). The secret vehicle of Vajrayāna.

milam bardo (rMi.lam bar.do). The transitional state of dreams.

mudrā (Phyag.rgya). Gesture.

nāga (kLu.) A kind of supernatural being.

Nirmānakāya (sPrul.sku). Unobstructed miraculous emanation form.

Nyingma (rNying.ma). The original full Sūtra and Mantrayāna teachings which first flourished expansively in Tibet.

nyugma'i yeshe (gNyug.ma'i ye.shes). The unending continuity of non-dualistic wisdom mind.

Orgyen Padma Jungnay (O.rgyan Pad.ma 'Byung.gnas). Padmasambhava: Guru Rinpoche, born from a lotus in Oddiyana.

parinirvāṇa (Mya.ngan las 'das.pa). The passage into the state of enlightenment.

rangzhin bardo (Rang.bzhin bar.do). The transitional state of life between birth and death.

Rūpakāya (gZugs.sku). The immeasurable embodiment of pure form; both Nirmānakāya and Sambhogakāya.

sādhana (sGrub.thabs). Method of accomplishing general or supreme siddhi.

samādhi (bSam.gtan). Meditation.

Samantabhadra (Kun.tu.bzang.po). The Dharmakāya Buddha.

samaya (Dam.tshig). Tantric promise.

Sambhogakāya (Longs.sku). Immeasurable qualities of flawless, inconceivable, desireless exaltation form.

saṃsāra ('Khor.ba). Cyclic existence; the projections created by dualistic mind.

samten bardo (bSam.gten bar.do). The transitional state of meditation.

Sangha (dGe.'dun). Those who practice virtue on the path of Dharma.

Saraswatī (dByang.chan.ma). The wisdom goddess of unobstructed knowing who is the consort of Mañjúsrī.

Śakyamuni. The Buddha Śakyamuni.

śāstra ('Grel.pa). Any Dharma, whether Sūtra or Mantrayāna, which originates directly from the Buddha's Dharma, revealed by the Buddha's followers.

sem kyi gyud (Sems kyi rgyud). Ordinary continuous mind that is obscured by delusion.

shūnyatā (sTong.pa nyid). Great emptiness.

siddhi (dNgos.grub). Accomplishment, including general accomplishment within substantial existence and supreme accomplishment which is enlightenment.

sidpa bardo (Srid.pa bar.do). The transitional state of the junction between past and future existences.

skandha (Phung.po). The five aggregates of form, feeling, perception, intention, and consciousness.

sūtra (mDo). The speech of Buddha according to the causal Hīnayāna and Mahāyāna teachings.

Sutranta (mDo.sde.pa). One of the two main categories of the Hīnayāna doctrine.

tantra (rGyud); tantric Buddhism. The three vehicles of the outer tantras of kriyā, upa, and yoga, and the three vehicles of the inner tantras of mahāyoga, anu yoga, and ati yoga.

Tārā. *See* Arya Tārā.

Tathāgata. Buddha.

tshenchay (mTshan.bchas). With characteristics.

tshenmed (mTshan.med). Without characteristics; insubstantial.

tulku ngepa medpa'i takpa (sPrul.sku nges.pa med.pa'i rtag.pa). The indefinite permanence of Nirmānakāya; the indefinite aspects of the infinite emanations of effortless compassion which can arise in any form, time, and direction, corresponding to the faculties of sentient beings.

upadeśa (Man.ngag). The pith of teachings.

Vajradhāra (rDo.rje 'Chhang). The deity who is the source of the three lineages of the spoken teachings of the tantras, which are the lineage of the transmission of the wisdom mind of the Buddhas, the lineage of the transmission by signs of the Vidyādharas, and the lineage by transmission of supreme individuals, transmitted in an unbroken lineage to one's guru.

Vajramaster (bLa.ma). *See* guru.

Vajrasattva (rDo.rje Sems.dpa'). The deity of indestructible wisdom.

Vajrayāna (Theg.pa chhen.po). The teaching of the great way of carrying from lower states to higher spiritual states.

Vajrayogini (rDo.rje rNal.'byor.ma). The ḍākinī of the union of wisdom and skillful means.

yāna (Theg.pa). Way of lifting up from lower states to higher spiritual states.

Yeshe Tshogyal (Ye.shes mTsho.rgyal). The wisdom ḍākinī who is the emanation of Saraswatī and the main consort and lineage holder of Guru Rinpoche.

yogācāra (Sems.tsam.pa). One of the two main categories of the Mahāyāna doctrine.

yoga tantra (rNal.'byor rgyud). One of the three outer tantras.

yogi; yogini (rNal.'byor, rNal.'byor.ma). Male and female practitioners of the path of union.